FAITH In Radiant Color

WALKING UNDER THE
RAINBOW OF GOD'S PROMISES

WILLIAM A. HEIMBAUGH

CLAY BRIDGES
PRESS

Faith in Radiant Color
Walking under the Rainbow of God's Promises

Published by Clay Bridges in Houston, TX
www.claybridgespress.com

ISBN 978-1-953300-77-5 (paperback)
ISBN 978-1-953300-76-8 (ebook)

Special Sales: Most Clay Bridges titles are available in special quantity discounts. Custom imprinting or excerpting can also be done to fit special needs. For standard bulk orders, go to www.claybridgesbulk.com. For specialty press or large orders, contact Clay Bridges at info@claybridgespress.com.

In Loving Memory of

Tina Heimbaugh

An Inspiration to All

Table of Contents

Acknowledgments

There are many people to thank for making this book a reality. They include my late wife, Tina; my current wife, Cindy; my sons, Andrew and Grant; my sister-in-law, Kim; my in-laws, David and Wanda; numerous prayer warriors and friends; and my primary editor, Jenny Marta. They provided the encouragement and prayer support to enable me to tell this incredible story.

Although these people were instrumental in the development of this book, the simple fact is that all glory and thanksgiving should be given to God. He was the one who charted the course traveled by His faithful servant Tina Heimbaugh. He was the one who equipped and encouraged Tina as she repeatedly sought Him for guidance and direction during her journey. He was the one who comforted and sustained all of us who witnessed the journey. He was the one who gave me the perseverance and strength to document the story long after her death. Yes, it all begins and ends with our Heavenly Father and our Lord and Savior, Jesus Christ.

Preface

Wouldn't it be wonderful if we were so filled with God's Spirit and the abiding Word of God that we were like those lights that automatically come on at night or even when a shadow of darkness covers their sensors during the day? What if we were so sensitive to the Holy Spirit that within us there was a spiritual light that would turn on even when our enemy's shadow of darkness came into our midst? What if we started viewing things through a spiritual lens and observing things that previously we could not see because our focus was elsewhere?

That spiritual light was turned on in someone who was very close to me. This book chronicles "God moments" that occurred in the life of my first wife, Tina Heimbaugh. The vast majority of these events, which occurred during the last 14 years of her life, cannot be explained other than through divine intervention. Although some may say these events have been glamorized or simply did not happen, I can testify that all of them did occur since they were witnessed by me, family members, friends, healthcare professionals, and other people. These miracles can only be attributed to the handiwork of God. In fact, the stories detailed in this book are really God's story as lived out by one of His servants on earth.

I do not pretend to understand everything in this book. At the time of their occurrence, I simply observed and made mental notes to myself. However, after the frequency of these events increased, my spiritual eyes were opened, and I began to view things from a new perspective.

> *But when anything is exposed by the light, it becomes visible, for anything that becomes visible is light. Therefore it says,*
>
> *"Awake, O sleeper,*
> *and arise from the dead,*
> *and Christ will shine on you."*
>
> —Eph. 5:13–14 ESV

For those who say miracles never happen anymore, I simply say . . . read on.

Introduction

God speaks very clearly . . . even through rainbows.

Most of us go about our lives without really listening to God. Make no mistake, God communicates with us in various ways. It may be through a word from a friend, a phone call from a relative, a song on the radio, a question from your child, a pastor's sermon, an email from a business associate, a thoughtful gesture from a neighbor, or even a seemingly random thought in your mind. Although God uses these and many other ways to communicate with us, His approach with Tina was more direct. Simply stated, God spoke to her in a highly visual manner using rainbows—most notably, double rainbows.

Before June 1995, I had never seen a double rainbow, much less a perfect, end-to-end double rainbow that was completely filled in with vibrant colors. As of this writing, I have now witnessed many rainbows, single and double. They have included the awe-inspiring ecstasies in the sky, as well as rainbows on walls, calendars, clocks, puzzles, and jewelry. These calling cards from God, which served as Tina's road map during her journey, made me more aware of what is going on around me. No longer will I be oblivious to the many signs and wonders that occur all the time in God's creation.

I don't know why God chose rainbows to communicate with Tina, but I am glad He did. His visual promises have strengthened my faith and given me a zest for Him that could only have been authored by God Himself. God's use of rainbows in Tina's life has definitely underscored the Bible verses that were given to her during her initial cancer diagnosis. "'For I know the plans I have for you,' declares the LORD, 'plans to prosper you and not to harm you, plans to give you hope and a future. Then you will call on me and come and pray to me, and I will listen to you. You will seek me and find me when you seek me with all your heart'" (Jer. 29:11–13).

Tina lived out her faith on a daily basis and never missed an opportunity to spread the gospel, regardless of her surroundings and physical condition. In conformity with the exhortation in Hebrews 12:1–2, she ran the race with perseverance that was marked out for her, with her eyes always fixed on Jesus. She lived out the identity change (put on the "new self") referred to by the Apostle Paul in the book of Colossians. "If then you have been raised in Christ, seek the things that are above, where Christ is, seated at the right hand of God. Set your minds on things that are above, not on things that are on earth. For you have died, and your life is hidden with Christ in God" (Col. 3: 1–3 ESV).

Tina succumbed to a physical death in 2008. However, the death of her old mind and spirit occurred in 1995, and, more importantly, her evolution to a "new creation" commenced shortly thereafter. It seemed God had other plans for her. God wanted to use her to help tell *His* story.

1

Pushed by an Angel

There are four things in life that are guaranteed to cause stress for most people: (1) changing jobs, (2) moving to a new town, (3) raising children, and (4) making new friends in a place where you feel totally isolated. Unfortunately, Tina and I experienced all these things in January 1995. I had just taken a new job with an engineering company in Tyler, Texas. After working 10 years with an industrial water treatment company in Houston, Texas, I felt it was time to move on and start a new chapter in my life. Although I don't think Tina was ready to move yet, she knew this day was coming since I had been preparing her for nearly two years. The thought of raising our two young children in a small-town setting in East Texas was appealing. However, the move meant detaching ourselves from the familiar surroundings of Nassau Bay, Texas, and the greater Houston area. The move would also mean that my wife would have to quit her job as an advertising consultant and desktop publisher.

The departure from Tina's old life turned out to be more painful for her than I had anticipated. She really liked the advertising business and was a natural in the sales and marketing arena due to her interpersonal skills, persuasiveness, and business savvy. Her advertising consulting business gave her the opportunity to meet people, make money, and have fun. It also connected her with the local businesses and political landscape. Therefore, a move to a new city four hours away would require her to say goodbye to all of that. Nonetheless, when I said I was ready to move, she terminated her advertising consulting business and sold the newsletter she had started two years earlier.

The move from Houston to Tyler required removing our oldest child, Andrew, from a Montessori school that he dearly loved and enrolling him in a new school where he would have no friends and a new teacher. We also had a two-year-old son, Grant, who would need a new childcare facility. The move would require both boys to make an adjustment in their lives. Of course, not only would our kids have to make significant adjustments in terms of surroundings and friends, but we would also have to adjust. The move would require Tina to meet new people, leave her only relative within a short driving distance, seek out a new job, find a new church home, and, if that were not enough, adjust to a new life that would basically require her to live as a single parent while I traveled extensively in a new business development job. Understandably, she was stressed.

My initial plan was to rent a house in Tyler until our home in Nassau Bay sold. That would make the financial situation a lot easier and give me time to make sure the job worked out before we made the commitment of buying a new home. For whatever reason, the rental market for homes in Tyler was almost nonexistent. It seemed there were few homes for rent in the size we needed. After scouring the rental market for several weeks, we finally found a home we could tolerate. It was significantly smaller than the home we left in Houston, which meant the garage became the storage closet. The house also had a strange layout. The kitchen was in the front of the house and blocked any light from entering the living room. To say the least, it was the darkest home I had ever been in. Nonetheless, it was our home, and we attempted to make the best of it.

It didn't take long for the rigors of the new environment in Tyler to take hold. I was gone at least two to four nights a week, which was a constant reminder that my wife was by herself the majority of the time. That was a real change for her since none of my previous jobs had required overnight travel. It meant that nearly all the daily tasks of childrearing were now left up to her. The loss of contact with the business world was also unsettling. No longer did she have the opportunity to engage in business activities and nurture her social skills. She was now a full-time mom living in a new town. Since neither my wife nor I had any family members or close friends within 250 miles of Tyler, we did not have the luxury, like many parents, to drop the kids off at Grandma's house or leave them with another relative when Tina needed a break. She was immersed in a daily struggle of raising two young children in a dark house that felt like a tomb and making sure the older one got to and from school safely. With no outlet for interaction, she struggled in this environment.

To help get our family plugged in to the local community in Tyler, my wife enrolled our oldest son in piano lessons. Tina was an accomplished pianist, so getting Andrew involved with music at an early age seemed like a good thing to do. It would also allow her to socialize with people she was comfortable with. Interestingly, almost every Tuesday as they came home from piano lessons, Tina said they saw a rainbow in the sky. Even Andrew took note of these weekly panoramic displays of color and commented, "Mom, we always see a rainbow when we come home from piano lessons. I've never seen so many rainbows." Little did I know then the role rainbows would play in my wife's future. For now, it seemed like a visual oddity that occurred on a weekly basis to brighten her day.

Tina's first break from the daily routine occurred in June when she and the kids accompanied me on a business trip to Beaumont, Texas. This was the first time Tina had ever traveled with me for work. While I made sales calls during the day, Tina and the boys enjoyed time in the hotel swimming pool. During the second night of our stay, I insisted that we all go out to a nice place for dinner. The restaurant was a steak and seafood eatery in a one-story building on the west side of Beaumont. The meal was nice, and the evening was relatively peaceful. When we finished eating, Tina politely excused herself, and she and the boys made their way to the bathroom while I waited at the table and paid the bill. Twenty minutes passed, and the trio had not returned from the bathroom. Sensing something might be wrong, I summoned a waiter and asked if someone could check on a woman and two small boys in the women's bathroom. After several minutes, a restaurant employee informed me that my wife had fallen down the stairs and was in significant pain. I quickly exited the dining room and headed toward the front of the restaurant. Along the way I kept wondering, *What stairs could there be in a single-story building?* As it turned out, the bathrooms in this restaurant were in a small loft area that required you to climb a flight of stairs.

I finally saw Tina, who was in considerable pain. Fighting back tears, she told me that after leaving the bathroom, the heel of one of her shoes caught on the edge of a step, and she immediately started to lunge forward. Instinctively, she grabbed the railing as she started to tumble down the stairs. As she tried to catch herself, her ankle turned as the rest of her body went into an awkward position. She ended up falling down several steps. Tina said her pulse was racing and her ankle and chest muscles cried out in pain as she lay on the floor. Restaurant employees quickly came to her aid and moved her to a bench in the front hallway. Upon hearing Tina's recollection of the fall and examining her ankle, it was obvious to me that this injury might take a while to heal.

Since Tina had fallen on restaurant property and possibly injured herself seriously, the restaurant manager insisted that we go to the hospital and get her checked out. After initially resisting, we gave in, and I took Tina to a hospital close to our hotel. They took a few X-rays to make sure there were no broken bones and concluded that she had probably twisted her ankle and pulled several muscles in her chest. In the absence of any serious injuries, she was released from the hospital. It was late when we arrived back at the hotel that night.

Tina did not do anything the next day. Her whole body was sore. All she did was lie in bed and try to corral the kids. Of course, that was easier said than done. When I finished the last of my business meetings that day, I went to the hotel, picked up Tina and the boys, and made the four-hour trip back to Tyler.

The next day, as Tina was rubbing her sore shoulder, she noticed a pea-sized bump at the top of her right breast. Although the bump was in the same area where many of her chest muscles had been twisted and bruised during the fall, Tina felt there was something different about the bump. It was large enough to be viewed with the naked eye and was relatively firm. She said it did not feel like an injured muscle. It also did not feel or look like swelling or inflammation that typically surfaces on the skin after a fall. No, Tina was convinced this bump was unique.

When I arrived home from work that night, Tina told me about the mysterious bump. After looking at the bump, I concluded that it was most likely related to the fall. That obviously made sense due to the sequence of events. It would seem unlikely that a bump would just show up unless something had triggered it. Although the reasoning certainly seemed logical, Tina was still not convinced.

The following week we went to see an orthopedic doctor in Tyler for a follow-up visit, as recommended by the hospital staff in Beaumont. We had no primary care physician since we were new to Tyler, so we had to get an appointment with a doctor Tina had never seen before. The doctor reviewed Tina's case and the X-rays we brought with us from Beaumont. More X-rays were taken, and they confirmed the absence of any broken bones. The orthopedist did perform a physical examination of the bump on Tina's breast but said there was probably nothing to worry about. He declined to order a biopsy or any additional testing of the bump since that was not within the scope of his expertise. When we inquired about getting a mammogram, the orthopedist said it would not show anything since the breast tissue of a 33-year-old woman was too dense for a mammogram to be meaningful. The doctor then recommended some physical therapy exercises to speed recovery of her strained muscles and swollen ankle. He indicated that more healing time was necessary and cautioned Tina to be patient while her body recovered from the trauma of the fall. Tina was obviously frustrated by the lack of information and diagnostic assistance regarding the bump. As we left the doctor's office, she told the orthopedist, "I don't believe you. I think there is more to the story."

A few days later, Tina went to an imaging center to see if she could get a mammogram. The technologist on staff indicated the clinic did not perform mammograms on females younger than 35 without a doctor's order due to breast tissue density. Tina explained that the bump on her breast could be felt by anyone who examined her and not following up on such visual evidence seemed illogical and not within the spirit of providing medical care. After a passionate plea and proclamation from Tina that she was not going to leave the clinic until she received a mammogram, the imaging center staff relented and agreed to perform the mammogram. They called the next day and said, "We don't see anything, and there is nothing to worry about." Once again, Tina retorted, "I don't believe you!" She then advised me that we were going back to Houston to see her obstetrician/gynecologist (OB/GYN) to see if he could help decipher the "bump mystery."

Three weeks later, we arrived at the office of Tina's OB/GYN in Houston. It was apparent he was not overly enthusiastic about seeing us. He didn't understand why we would consult a physician whose primary expertise was female reproductive health, pregnancy, and childbirth, especially after we had already seen an orthopedic doctor. It seemed as if we had violated the physician's chain of command by seeking another opinion. We were only seeking an opinion from someone who knew us and would hopefully take a genuine interest in assessing the bump on Tina's breast. To our amazement, the doctor shared with us the same response as the orthopedic doctor—a mammogram would not help in this situation due to the density of the breast tissue and that the bump was most likely the body's physical response to the fall. Upon examination of Tina's breast, he opined that the bump was probably not breast cancer and Tina should consider taking vitamin E for six months to see if it would disappear. Despite our insistence, he declined to order a biopsy of the bump. We were unsure if this was because it was really his medical opinion or if perhaps he knew that insurance would not pay for this type of examination. I offered to pay for the biopsy, but that didn't change his response. In any case, we were shocked that he and the previous doctors were convinced there was nothing to worry about. Once again, Tina proclaimed, "I don't believe you. I know something is wrong."

As we walked out of the OB/GYN's office, it was hard to digest that we were now zero for three in getting a diagnosis that made sense to us regarding the mysterious bump. I kept thinking, *Why didn't they just sample and test the bump, especially if I was willing to pay for it and had just driven four hours to get to the doctor's office?* As an engineer, I was baffled by the lack of a scientific approach. Tina was infuriated and frustrated. When your body tells you there is something wrong and you seek medical help, you expect the necessary tests and examinations to be performed to diagnose the problem. You also expect the results to be delivered to you in an empathetic, non-patronizing manner. It seemed Tina received none of this. All she kept getting was "there is nothing to worry about" and "you need to calm down and let your body heal."

None of the doctors we had consulted over the course of a month seemed to have a grasp of my wife's perseverance to get to the bottom of the situation. As we walked out of the doctor's office in Houston, my wife quipped, "An angel pushed me down those stairs for a reason, and now I need to find out why!" As I looked into Tina's face, it was as if God were speaking directly to me. Tina spoke with such conviction, and her eyes were like laser beams into my soul. I acknowledged her passion to get to the bottom of her physical condition, and for the first time, I realized there may be a lot more to this story than meets the eye.

2

My wife and I were blessed to have some dear friends when we lived in Houston in the late 1980s and early 1990s. Two of them went to our same church in Nassau Bay. They were Grant's godparents and also in our same life group at church. We got to know them on a very personal level and stayed in touch with them after we moved to Tyler. The woman was a nurse and worked at the Texas Medical Center (TMC) in Houston. She routinely worked alongside some of the finest doctors in the country in the surgical wing of one of the TMC hospitals. When we relayed our frustrating story regarding Tina's bump, she quickly inserted herself into our situation and indicated she would get us an appointment with a specialist.

The following week, we had an appointment with a world-renowned breast surgeon with an extraordinary résumé. She was extremely professional and had a dry sense of humor. Her qualifications were impeccable, and we could sense that this doctor would quickly get to the bottom of Tina's situation. She reviewed the X-rays and the information we brought with us.

She just shook her head when we told her that previous medical opinions indicated there was nothing to worry about and that a biopsy of the bump was never performed. She responded, "The guesswork will stop here." When we asked how many young women get breast cancer, she responded that more than a third of her patients were Tina's age or younger. That was a wake-up call for us since we had been led to believe this was a disease primarily associated with older women.

As much as we were frustrated by a lack of information and scientific approach during our previous doctor visits, we were ecstatic and relieved over the can-do attitude of this surgeon. She methodically performed a physical examination of Tina's breasts and ordered tests with a sense of urgency. Nurses, colleagues, and support personnel snapped to attention as the doctor barked out orders in military-like fashion. When Tina asked if a biopsy of the bump would be performed, the doctor said without hesitation, "Yes," and gave us a look as if to say, *Why wouldn't it?* We quickly realized this was a world-class professional who was admired by her peers and subordinates in the medical community. Her thorough examination of laboratory data and charts quickly gave us the comfort that no stone would be unturned. She spoke with authority and conducted her business with an efficiency I had never seen before. She laid out a plan based on a comprehensive approach that left little to chance. The path forward would include a mammogram and a fine-needle biopsy.

The mammogram, which was performed first, revealed sufficient evidence to warrant further investigation. The fine-needle biopsy was next. To my surprise, the biopsy procedure would be performed in the surgeon's office later that afternoon so no time would be lost and the results could be expedited. Once again, we were amazed and relieved how quickly things were coming together. It seemed we were going to get more information regarding the mysterious bump in one afternoon than in all the previous doctors' visits combined.

The time arrived for the fine-needle biopsy. The environment was calm, and our waiting was kept to a minimum. The ultrasound and fine-needle biopsy team quickly gathered. The surgeon explained the procedure to us to ensure we knew what the test would show and not show. After our approval to proceed, Tina received pain medication and numbing cream to her chest area. The surgeon then guided the needle to several carefully selected locations, including the bump. Samples were taken at each site specified by the surgeon. It was apparent to me that the surgeon was seeking clarity on other areas as well, not just the bump located at the top of Tina's right breast. I silently thanked her for the thoroughness of her exploratory effort. She indeed was seeking a complete picture of Tina's breast region. Although the procedure seemed relatively simple, great care was taken to only move the needle a small amount to minimize any pain and any unnecessary tearing of the breast tissue. As a result, the procedure took almost an hour to complete to the surgeon's satisfaction.

The doctor seemed pleased with the samples taken from Tina's body. They were then sent to a laboratory for a complete pathology workup. The surgeon advised that it would take a few days for the lab work to be completed. She told us to be accessible by phone if we were traveling anywhere. Although her medical ethics would not allow her to voice a preliminary opinion, I sensed that she knew there was an undesirable growth in Tina's body.

As we left the doctor's office that day, we pondered what the path forward might be. Our minds wandered as we considered the range of possibilities. That night we prayed for Tina's health and for a definitive diagnosis so the proper next steps could be performed, if needed. Of course, we also prayed that all the samples taken from the fine-needle biopsy would be benign. Although this moment in time was scary for both of us, we were comforted by the fact that the surgeon was in control of the medical evaluation. We also rested in the knowledge that God was ultimately in control of the situation and would dictate what would happen next.

3

God Spoke

Tina and the boys went to Tina's parents' home in rural Missouri while we waited for the results of the fine-needle biopsy. Although this was a summer vacation that had been planned prior to Tina's fall and subsequent doctor visits, the timing of the trip was definitely a godsend. Her parents would be able to provide her with emotional and spiritual support when she received the test results. They could also care for the boys in case Tina needed to leave quickly for medical reasons.

Hours seemed like days while we waited for the results. Three days later, Tina got the phone call from the surgeon, who did not mince words and reported that *Tina had breast cancer.* She admitted that she was surprised with the results based on Tina's excellent health and lack of a significant history of cancer in the family (only one paternal grandmother had had breast cancer). The surgeon ended the call by simply saying, "Just tell me how I can help when you're ready." Obviously, the surgeon knew Tina would need time to process the information. Her word choice also suggested that a path forward needed to be developed soon.

After the call ended, Tina and her parents huddled in prayer. Overwhelmed by uncertainty and fear, Tina passed out in her father's arms. She regained consciousness a few minutes later on the living room floor. As she looked at her parents' faces and saw their somber mood, she realized the unsettling news she had received from the breast surgeon was not a dream. Cancer was now a permanent part of her life. Tina's mind began to wander as she mentally explored this new reality. The life she knew just moments before was over. One phone call changed everything: *Life before cancer—life with cancer.* She focused on the fact that she was only 33 years old, had a husband working at a new job, and two young boys ages 7 and 2. Her mind began to contemplate things—*What are the next steps? How do I communicate this message to my husband and children? What does all of this mean?*

Thankfully, Tina was raised in a Christian home and her life was built on a foundation of faith. After hearing the news, Tina's mother immediately called a neighbor who in turn called one of her friends, a prayer warrior named Patsy. The ladies prayed over the phone as they interceded on Tina's behalf. Patsy then asked Tina if she and her husband could come to her parents' home to pray for her in person. Without hesitation, Tina welcomed the request.

Tina always believed what the Bible told her about many things. Although she didn't know a lot about God and what He was capable of doing, she was now seeing the hands and feet of Christ in action. Patsy and her husband came to her parents' home, laid hands on Tina, and anointed her with oil. They prayed for her and spoke God's words of life over her from the Bible. They emphasized that "faith comes from hearing, and hearing through the word of Christ" (Rom. 10:17 ESV). Patsy then gave Tina a Scripture that God had given her at 4:00 that morning as she was praying for her. God told her the following verses were Tina's Scriptures for her cancer journey: "'For I know the plans I have for you,' declares the Lord, 'plans to prosper you and not to harm you, plans to give you hope and a future. Then you will call on me and come and pray to me, and I will listen to you. You will seek me and find me when you seek me with all your heart'" (Jer. 29:11–13).

After the prayer intercessors left, Tina distinctly remembered Patsy saying, "My people perish for a lack of knowledge." Tina knew then it was time for her to call on God for wisdom and knowledge. She immediately opened her Bible, and with a mustard seed of faith planted in her, she began to study the healing stories in the Gospel of Luke. As she immersed herself in the Bible, she began to feel a glimmer of hope inside. In fact, she started believing at that moment that God was going to give her a sign that He was going to perform miracles in her life.

Tina studied her Bible with great excitement for the remainder of the day. Although the learning she gained from this in-depth examination of the Bible was new to her, she was determined to find out how God healed people. The more she studied the Bible that afternoon, the more her faith grew. A calming peace enveloped her as she continued her methodical review of Luke and other Bible passages related to healing. She sensed that God was ready to give her a sign and that He would direct her path forward.

As Tina's expectations for a heavenly sign grew, a storm arrived on this perfectly clear, hot summer day. The storm was unexpected based on the prevailing weather forecasts. The sun and elevated ambient temperature quickly gave way to cooler temperatures, wind, and rain. After the storm passed, Tina looked out one of the windows in front of the house. A beautiful sunset was visible on the horizon. As Tina was gazing at the sunset and reflecting on the Bible passages she had read earlier that afternoon, she suddenly heard a loud voice. It was her mother yelling, "Oh my goodness! Look out the back window!" Tina raced to the back of the house and looked out the dining room window. She could not believe her eyes. In the southern sky just a few hundred yards from the back porch was the most brilliant and perfect double rainbow resting over the cornfield. It was absolutely stunning with no obstructions, perfect from beginning to end. Both rainbows glowed with such brilliance.

Immediately, Tina knew that the majestic double rainbow was just for her from the King of Glory. As she stood and watched the awe-inspiring artwork in the sky, the bottom portion of the rainbow filled in with the color purple as if God had taken a paintbrush and filled in the color between the cornfield and the sky under the rainbow. As Tina and her parents stood and watched the beautiful panoramic display, all Tina could do was tremble from this mighty display of divine power. Yes, God was speaking directly to her through His creation. She knew at that moment God was in control of her situation. She had asked for a sign from God, and He had delivered. Not only had God given Tina the double rainbow, He had also given her the following verses that provided her with hope and comfort:

- "'For I know the plans I have for you,' declares the LORD, 'plans to prosper you and not to harm you, plans to give you hope and a future'" (Jer. 29:11).
- "I, even I, am the LORD, and apart from me there is no savior" (Isa. 43:11).
- "The fear of the Lord is a fountain of life, turning a person from the snares of death" (Prov. 14:27).

- "A heart at peace gives life to the body, but envy rots the bones" (Prov. 14:30).
- "The eyes of the Lord are everywhere, keeping watch on the wicked and the good. The soothing tongue is a tree of life, but a perverse tongue crushes the spirit" (Prov. 15:3–4).

Later that afternoon, Tina called me with the results of the biopsy. However, before I could even process the unsettling information, she started telling me about this beautiful double rainbow that appeared in the sky over her parents' backyard. She was overwhelmed with excitement that God had given her a distinct sign that He was in control of her journey. She recounted how a prayer chain was started immediately in response to the cancer news and that prayer warriors had prayed over her and anointed her with oil. She relayed the healing passages that God had given her during her Bible study that afternoon and how those same passages were confirmed to her through phone calls she received from friends and relatives. Little did I know then that my wife would use her new situation in life as a means to proclaim the gospel. For now, she was focused on the positive aspects of her new spiritual journey and not on the cancer diagnosis. It seemed as if she had taken lemons and turned them into lemonade.

As I hung up the phone, my mind began wandering all over the place. My wife had just told me she has breast cancer. If that were not enough to grasp, she also conveyed a sense of peace and spiritual excitement that I had never witnessed before. Perhaps this was "the peace that passes all understanding" referenced in the Bible. In any case, I was unsure how to balance the cancer news with God's affirmation of the double rainbow. As I made the walk to my boss's office to inform him of the news I had just received, I struggled with how I would convey the message. Do I just say, "My wife has breast cancer and I need to take some time off," or do I blend it with the story about a sign from God and how the hands and feet of Christ were evident? As I entered my boss's office, he looked up from his desk and could see that something was troubling me. I could not speak for a few minutes. However, a calming presence came over me, and I simply said, "Have you ever seen a double rainbow?" He looked puzzled with my opening query. I then relayed the breast cancer news along with the rainbow sighting and the spiritual confirmations my wife had received that day.

4

Confirming the Path Forward

The day after God's calling card in the sky, Tina scheduled a consultation with the surgeon in Houston for the following week. Upon arriving in Houston, she called an emergency prayer meeting with people from our old church. Nearly all who were contacted dropped what they were doing and attended the impromptu prayer meeting. I made the trip from Tyler to Houston and also joined the meeting. One of the prayer warriors at the church led the session and allowed each person an opportunity to lay hands on Tina and pray over her. The leader spoke with such conviction and offered up several verses that God had given her. Other people voiced prayers that God had given them. All spoke with immeasurable passion and asked God to provide His veil of protection over Tina and a clear path forward regarding her treatment. As each of the prayers was offered up, I felt Tina's body temperature rise. Her skin seemed to glow, and a smile was on her face. Her warming physical condition and emotional appearance gave me comfort I could not explain.

The prayer meeting was the first time in my life I had sensed the powerful impact of prayer.

After the prayer meeting, I asked Tina how she was feeling since this was the first time I had seen her in person since she received the cancer news. She said she was anxious regarding the next steps. She said she had been reading her Bible, and the Lord had spoken to her through the words in Hebrews 11:1: "Now faith is confidence in what we hope for and assurance about what we do not see." I told her I had felt such warmth during the prayer meeting and that God would indeed reveal the next steps for her treatment through the surgeon.

That night, Tina and I prayed together regarding a path forward. The specific issue on the table was the extent of surgery required to remove the cancer cells in her right breast. Would a lumpectomy be sufficient to address her situation, or would a modified radical mastectomy be required to ensure removal of all cancer cells? The thought of removing part of Tina's body in either scenario was unpleasant to say the least. We decided to take the issue to the Lord once again. We asked God to make the decision for us because He was the only one who really knew what Tina needed. While we were praying, Tina kept reciting the words God had given her during the impromptu prayer meeting: "Seek wisdom, knowledge and understanding; it will guard your life." She followed this with the familiar words from Philippians 4:6–7: "Do not be anxious about anything, but in every situation, by prayer and petition, with thanksgiving, present your requests to God. And the peace of God, which transcends all understanding, will guard your hearts and your minds in Christ Jesus."

The next day we made the trip to the surgeon's office for the follow-up consultation. To our surprise, the surgeon recommended a modified radical mastectomy, not a lumpectomy. Apparently, a second cancerous area was discovered during the ultrasound and fine-needle biopsy. Not only was the original bump problematic, but a second area was also of concern. The surgeon indicated that normally there is only one area where the cancer cells are concentrated within the breast. However, in Tina's case, there were two areas, and they were independent of each other. This unusual cancer cell mapping made it a more complex situation. Based on the two areas, the doctor recommended the more aggressive surgical approach—removing the entire breast rather than just part of it.

As the doctor was relaying her recommendation for a mastectomy and the justification for it, I recalled that the surgeon had taken her time when she performed the fine-needle biopsy. Thank goodness she was thorough! If only the bump had been biopsied, the other area of her breast would have gone undetected and untreated. The words given to Tina by God earlier that day regarding "seek wisdom and knowledge" came immediately to the forefront. Yes, God was guarding her life by utilizing the wisdom and knowledge of this highly trained surgeon.

Two days later, Tina was admitted to the hospital for a modified radical mastectomy. It was August 1, 1995. It was also our youngest son's birthday. But instead of celebrating his third birthday, there we were in Houston preparing ourselves mentally for a procedure that no woman wants to undergo. Tina was very candid in her thoughts at that time. As she lay on the gurney waiting to be wheeled into the operating room, she said that everything that identified her as a person, or at least who she thought she was, was being stripped away. She literally had no clothes, jewelry, or makeup on. She was simply a fragile human being under God's complete control. However, she said knowing

God was in charge was very comforting because she trusted and believed Him and what He had told her.

The pathology results from the four-hour surgery indicated there were five cancerous areas in Tina's right breast—*not one, not two, but five!* It turned out that three of the areas were too small to be detected by the ultrasound and only one (the original bump) was visible to the naked eye. Unbelievably, none of the five cancer areas were the same type, according to the pathologist. Although the number of cancer sites was disturbing, the good news was that all the lymph nodes removed in the area around her right breast were clear. Thus, there was no involvement with the lymphatic system.

As I paused to reflect on the post-surgery news, I silently thanked God for giving Tina the courage and persistence to get to this point. Although she had to endure an intense surgical procedure and was now physically in a weakened state, she was definitely in a better place. In fact, without God "knocking on her door" and pushing her down some stairs, she might not even be here.

That evening, our dear friend who was responsible for coordinating the initial visit with the surgeon stopped by the hospital room to check on Tina. She brought a picture with her that her seven-year-old daughter had made. It was a rainbow with clouds at each end and a pot of gold underneath. The picture was obviously significant to Tina since God was speaking to her with rainbows. Tina immediately smiled at the sight of the rainbow and remarked that God even uses children to communicate to His people. It was not until seven months later that God would reveal to her the meaning of the rainbow and the pot of gold. While giving her testimony to a large gathering of worshippers at our former church in Nassau Bay, God directed Tina to the Scripture in 1 Peter 1:6: "In all this you greatly rejoice, though now for a little while you may have had to suffer grief in all kinds of trials."

Due to the intensity of the surgery, Tina stayed in the hospital for four days. Since the boys were still in Missouri, I was able to stay with her the entire time. She was in a lot of pain, and I did my best to provide emotional support. I read many passages of Scripture to her. She seemed to receive much comfort from the Bible passages, and I must admit that they seemed to be building up my faith as well. The nurses and hospital staff who were assigned to Tina were top-notch and extremely attentive to Tina's needs. Once again, I thanked the Lord for leading us to this place where wisdom and knowledge seemed to abound.

After Tina was discharged from the hospital, she continued her recovery at her sister's house in Houston. The surgeon wanted to keep Tina close by in case there were any complications from the surgery. After two weeks, Tina received the green light to go home. We then made the journey back to Tyler. Her parents brought our children back to us shortly after. We finally were a family again under the same roof.

5

Pointing the Way

After Tina had sufficiently healed from her surgery, it was time to move on to the next step in her treatment program. Our focus now turned to choosing an oncologist. Since we didn't know anything about oncologists and cancer treatment facilities in Tyler, we decided to go back to Houston to commence our search. Houston was familiar to us since we had lived there for 10 years. It also had an excellent reputation in the cancer treatment field. The combination of familiar surroundings and cancer expertise was comforting to us even though it would mean a four-hour drive to Houston on a regular basis for consultations and treatment. Once again, we turned to the Lord for guidance. We prayed that God would give us a sign to lead us to the right person.

After talking with several people we knew, including the surgeon and our dear friend who was a nurse, we scheduled an appointment with a doctor who had an excellent reputation. He was head of hematology and oncology at one of the clinics affiliated with the hospital where Tina had her mastectomy. As we entered the waiting room on the day of our appointment, we were unsure of what to expect or even what to inquire about. The receptionist spoke to us in a very calm manner and informed us that it might be a while before the doctor could see us. The waiting room was packed, and it was obvious the doctor was running behind schedule. However, none of the people in the waiting room seemed to mind the long wait. When we spoke to the people beside us, they acknowledged the waiting room was always full during their visits. However, they followed this observation by saying, "Don't worry. It is worth the wait. The doctor is excellent, and he will spend as much time with you as you need. Besides, where else do we have to go that is more important than this?" As we spoke to other people in the waiting room while we waited for our 4:00 p.m. appointment, it was apparent that every person there was comforted by knowing they would get their fair share of the oncologist's time.

Finally, we were called back to one of the examination rooms. Now our wait continued in a private setting as opposed to the main waiting room. As the clock approached 6:00 p.m., our minds began to wander again, and we openly discussed if we were really in the right place. It seemed the doctor had a huge patient load and was well respected by his peers. No doubt, the people in the waiting room thought this man was the best choice for them. However, did he really have the time to spend with us on a regular basis to make us feel important? Would his large patient load detract from Tina's case and developing a plan just for her? The longer we waited, the more questions entered our minds. Suddenly Tina exclaimed, "Look on the wall above the sink. There is a rainbow on that calendar!" I turned to look at the calendar, which was on the correct month of August 1995. Sure enough, there was a brilliant double rainbow on it! *Okay, Lord. Message received. We are in the right place!*

Seconds after the rainbow sighting on the wall calendar, the doctor walked in. He apologized for the long wait and asked what questions we had at this point of the process. After all the questions that had entered our mind just minutes earlier, we had difficulty coming up with just one. It seemed God had cleared our minds of any doubts and conveyed a message of peace with regard to this doctor.

The oncologist said he had reviewed Tina's case and had also talked with the surgeon. Based on his research and experience, he recommended chemotherapy for Tina, but not radiation. He said it was important to utilize a systemic approach first (chemotherapy) to make sure the cancer cells did not spread any further. He said radiation could be conducted down the road, but in his opinion, radiation was not appropriate at this time given the number of cancer sites that were discovered during the mastectomy and the proximity of those cells to the heart. It was obvious this doctor had done a lot of homework on Tina's case before we ever arrived for our consultation. In fact, he said that Tina's case was going to be followed closely within the research community due to the number of unique cancer sites that were discovered on her breast. He then outlined an aggressive three-drug treatment program that had a good track record on breast cancer cells similar to Tina's.

The oncologist also recommended a doctor in Tyler we could follow up with in regard to administering the chemotherapy (chemo). He said this doctor had trained under him, so he was extremely comfortable recommending her. We were pleased that the chemo would be administered and monitored in Tyler since that would cut down on trips to Houston. It would also provide us with a local medical interface in the event Tina experienced any problems. However, we insisted that the oncologist remain involved from an oversight standpoint. The oncologist said that would not be a problem. We were glad he would remain involved. After all, God had led us to him with the help of a rainbow.

6

Divine Family Care

Shortly before Tina started chemo, my employer asked me to take on a new business development role in the company. The position involved significant international travel. I was hesitant to accept this new assignment not knowing what impact the extended travel might have on Tina and, more importantly, my availability to help her in the event of a medical emergency. On the one hand, I didn't want to decline the position since I was still relatively new to the company and didn't want to jeopardize my future career with them. I also had to be cognizant that I had good medical insurance and that leaving the company would mean possible financial hardship caused by significant healthcare costs. On the other hand, I wanted to support my wife in whatever manner was necessary to ensure that her health came first. If that meant we needed to move back to Houston to be closer to premier healthcare facilities, then I needed to set aside any personal ambitions and do what was best for Tina and the family.

Tina could tell that I was struggling with the new job assignment I had been offered. We had several discussions regarding this topic and whether we needed to move back to Houston for medical reasons. After several days of praying about my employment situation, Tina said we should stay in Tyler and make the best of it. I must admit I was a little surprised at her response. In fact, I had already prepared myself mentally to move back to Houston. However, Tina said I should take the new assignment and see what happens. She said if the new job didn't work out for whatever reason, we could always move back to Houston. For the time being, she felt that God had her in the right location and with healthcare facilities she was comfortable with. So we agreed to stay in Tyler, and I accepted the new position at my company.

A few days later, Tina and I met the oncologist in Tyler who had been referred to us by the esteemed oncologist we met just a week earlier in Houston. The local oncologist seemed like a competent physician and acknowledged she had trained under our God-chosen doctor. We discussed the details of Tina's proposed chemotherapy program and our need for the Houston doctor to remain involved in an oversight role. Although she was somewhat protective of her turf, she agreed with the oversight requirement out of respect for her mentor. She then proceeded to convey a lot of general information regarding chemotherapy, including the need to have a second person available to transport Tina to and from the clinic. After answering our questions, she scheduled Tina to receive her first chemo treatment the following week.

In the days after our consultation with the local oncologist and prior to beginning chemo, Tina spent a considerable amount of time researching nutrition information. The oncologist had provided some general nutrition information, but Tina was looking for more specific food recommendations. She wanted to know which foods were best while undergoing cancer treatment and which foods to avoid. It seemed the typical American fare would not be appropriate to support her physical and mental health during this time. Finally, after sifting through an array of confusing information, she resorted to prayer. Within a few hours after she had prayed one afternoon for food guidance, the doorbell rang at our house. When Tina opened the front door, a man was standing there. He said, "Ma'am, I've got a truck full of fruits and vegetables out here. Do you want any?" Tina could not believe her eyes. Once again, God had answered her prayer. "Yes," Tina exclaimed. "I will take one basket of every fruit and vegetable you have." Tina was beaming as the man unloaded the fruits and vegetables from his truck and brought them into our house. "God cares about every detail of your life," she quipped. We then prayed for the man and his food delivery business. When the man learned of Tina's cancer diagnosis, he told us that we were the only house on our street he had stopped at that day. He said he had a feeling he was supposed to stop at our house for some reason. Tina simply smiled and said, "God brought you here."

Before long, Tina was in the rigors of an aggressive chemotherapy program that was scheduled for seven rounds. Each round or cycle would last 21 days. Tina's blood counts and energy level trended up and down depending on what day of the cycle she was in. During the first few days after the drugs were injected, her blood counts sharply decreased as the chemicals indiscriminately destroyed her blood cells. As a chemical engineer, it was hard to get my mind around the concept of killing good cells as well as bad cells. However, this systemic approach was the only way to address the problem globally. After the blood counts had crashed to their low point, which usually occurred during the first seven days, her counts started trending back up as the cycle progressed. By the time the 21 days were up, her counts were hopefully back to where they were prior to administering the drugs. If they were not, the start of the next round was delayed until the blood counts were in an acceptable range.

Tina lost her hair after round two of chemo. I am sure she felt less feminine due to the hair loss and having only one breast. However, she took the hair loss in stride and began a campaign to model fashionable headwear. It seemed she wore a different hat every day when she went outdoors. Sometimes she combined the hat with a scarf. I must admit her hats and accessories were quite creative, if not downright trend-setting. She received many compliments on her head and neck attire, many from people who couldn't tell she was going through cancer treatment.

It seemed God was now using Tina in a new role to encourage other women who were dealing with chemotherapy-induced hair loss. She seemed to embrace that role, and her Energizer Bunny personality once again came to the forefront. I enjoyed watching her encourage total strangers and fellow chemo patients regarding the use of hats, especially in the checkout lines of grocery stores. It seemed she could pick a cancer patient out of a crowd with little effort, even when there were no outward signs of a medical issue. I never quite understood her ability to do that. I just chalked it up to God and His need for Tina to minister to those around her.

When Tina was inside our house, she never wore a hat. The boys and I were so used to her having minimal hair that the sight of a balding woman was not in the least bit unsettling. I remember when people came to the house and saw Tina for the first time after she had begun her chemotherapy. They would get that deer-in-the-headlights look. I simply had to remind myself that her new look was not normal for them and some recalibration was probably necessary. Meanwhile, I thought the lack of a hairdo was kind of sexy. To say the least, it gave her a unique look and seemed to embolden her personality even more.

Eventually, Tina's hair came back as the chemo reached the latter stages. Interestingly, her hair came back a different color. Her former reddish-brown locks were now a salt-and-pepper color. I told Tina I was married to a beautiful new woman. It was hard to imagine that a 33-year-old woman really did look good in a color scheme normally associated with older people. She never seemed to mind the new hair color and never expressed a desire to change it to look younger. She said if God wanted her to have a salt-and-pepper hair color, she was in agreement with that. She said that her mother, a hair stylist, could always fix the hair color later if she had a change of heart. For now, she was focused on staying the course and finishing the chemo.

Tina's passion to see the chemotherapy program through to the end was clearly evident. She endured seven rounds of chemo and amazingly never had one sick day. It seemed God had her in the palm of His hand the whole time and made sure she was well enough to participate in daily activities. Fortunately, there were folks who helped out with various tasks while Tina was going through chemo. First and foremost, Tina's father, who had recently retired, came to Tyler and stayed for two to three weeks at a time to assist with daily chores. He helped with routine tasks such as cooking and cleaning. He even potty trained our youngest child during that time. Members from our new church in Tyler came by periodically and brought food. The pastor of our church also came and mowed our yard a few times. Even though I was fully capable of mowing the yard myself and doing other jobs, I quickly learned that it was always a good idea to accept help of any kind. People genuinely wanted to show their support by doing something for us. I also had to realize that God was probably calling them to assist in this manner. It seemed God definitely had a plan in place that utilized a team approach, and who was I to get in the way of that?

Tina finished her chemotherapy during the last week of December 1995. As I reflected back on the five months she had endured chemo, I realized I had not traveled internationally at all in my new job. After worrying about an intense travel schedule that would supposedly take me around the globe many times, my out-of-town business trips had been limited only to domestic locations. All the international projects were handled through phone calls or fax or addressed by local sales agents in those countries. Since I had no international travel during this time, I was able to attend nearly all of Tina's chemo sessions and doctors' appointments.

Lo and behold, my international travel schedule picked up significantly in January 1996. It was as if a light switch had been turned on. I routinely traveled to overseas destinations during the months that followed. The good news was that Tina's health was improving, and it seemed the cancer was in remission. I didn't know it at the time, but Tina confessed a few years later that she had prayed every night that I would not have to travel internationally while she was going through chemotherapy. Once again, God had answered her prayers and provided divine family care.

7

Rainbows and Radiation

In the winter of 1997, Tina felt a little pea-like bump on the incision site of her mastectomy. At first, she didn't think much of it but eventually became concerned enough that she asked her Tyler oncologist about it during a regularly scheduled visit. The doctor said she believed the bump was a stitch left from the mastectomy and was nothing to worry about. This conclusion seemed odd to me as nearly two years had passed since the surgery. If a stitch were really the problem, wouldn't Tina have felt a bump a lot sooner? I could tell Tina was also unconvinced regarding the doctor's response. As we left the doctor's office, it didn't take much discussion between us to acknowledge that we needed to get other medical opinions. After all, we had already been down a similar path a few years earlier regarding the need for testing and evaluation of a bump. If there was more to the story regarding the new bump, history suggested we needed to find out as soon as possible. As such, we scheduled consultations with the Houston oncologist and the surgeon who had performed the mastectomy.

After examining Tina's chest area around the incision site and checking her records, the Houston oncologist said he believed the bump was scar tissue and not symptomatic of a problem. He indicated that all her blood work was normal and there was nothing to suggest that any cancer cells were present. A subsequent visit with the esteemed surgeon didn't reveal anything of a problematic nature either. She said the bump was most likely a piece of fat tissue and did not warrant further investigation.

Even though all three doctors had a slightly different take on the composition of the bump, they all agreed there was nothing to be concerned about. Once again, however, I could sense that Tina thought something else was going on. She was hoping that one of the doctors would order a biopsy to provide a definitive diagnosis. However, all three had recommended otherwise. As we left the surgeon's office that day, Tina said she would continue to pray and ask the Lord to protect her.

Three years passed, and in 2000, Tina convinced the breast surgeon to take a biopsy of the bump. Although the surgeon was still skeptical that the extremely small bump was little more than fat tissue, she ordered a fine-needle biopsy to assess the situation. While we were waiting for the pathology results in the doctor's office a few days later, we met another patient and her husband. Tina began sharing her testimony with them about how God was using rainbows to communicate with her. Upon hearing her story, the patient's husband asked Tina if she knew where the remainder of the rainbow was. Tina replied that she did not. He then told us the complete rainbow—the complete circle—is located in the throne room. He pointed out that we only see half of it. He told her to open her Bible and read the latter part of the first chapter of Ezekiel.

> *And above the expanse over their heads there was the likeness of a throne, in appearance like sapphire; and seated above the likeness of a throne was a likeness with a human appearance. And upward from what had the appearance of his waist I saw as it were gleaming metal, like the appearance of fire enclosed all around. And downward from what had the appearance of his waist I saw as it were the appearance of fire, and there was brightness around him. Like the appearance of the bow that is in the cloud on the day of rain, so was the appearance of the brightness all around. Such was the appearance of the likeness of the glory of the* LORD. *And when I saw it, I fell on my face, and I heard the voice of one speaking.*
>
> —Ezek. 1:26–28 ESV

Shortly after the rainbow discussion in the waiting room, the surgeon called us back to relay the results of the biopsy. She informed us that the pea-sized bump was not fat *but cancer.* The surgeon then proceeded to tell us that we needed to remove the bump right away. Further, she said that Tina would likely have to have the lymph nodes under her sternum biopsied and potentially removed. This startling news took us by complete surprise since the bump was extremely small. Was it really possible that cancer cells in such a small area previously mistaken as a stitch, scar tissue, or a piece of fat could have migrated to the sternum area? Obviously, we were not in a position to take a wait-and-see approach. After receiving our authorization to do whatever was surgically necessary to minimize the spread of any cancer cells, the surgeon removed the bump that was located at the original incision site. Fortunately, the pathology results of the excised bump indicated the cancer cells were isolated. Lab results on all samples taken around the incision site yielded clear margins. As a result, the lymph nodes under Tina's sternum did not have to be biopsied or removed.

After the surgery, the doctor indicated that the bump she removed from Tina's chest was highly unusual and did not follow typical protocol. She indicated that Tina's intuition regarding the bump had been a true blessing. If the cancer diagnosis had been made at a later point in time, the cancer cells would have likely spread to her lymphatic system.

A few weeks after the bump was removed, Tina scheduled a visit with her Tyler oncologist who recommended radiation as a supplemental treatment and put us in touch with a local radiation oncologist. He was emphatic about the need to do radiation. Although we appreciated his knowledge and expertise, we needed to weigh the pros and cons of such an approach. On the one hand, there was a need to be proactive and kill any remaining cancer cells that might be in Tina's chest. On the other hand, the field of radiation they were recommending was quite large and dangerously close to the heart. We wondered if they really could contain the radiation to the area they had projected. If the radiation was not sufficiently contained, the potential for unwanted cell destruction in other vital areas was a real possibility. Once again, it was time to take the matter to the Lord.

Tina fervently prayed and asked God to reveal the truth about what really needed to be done. Minutes before being summoned by clinic personnel so the radiation boundary lines could be marked on her chest, the Lord gave Tina the Scripture from Psalm 16:6–8: "The boundary lines have fallen for me in pleasant places; surely I have a delightful inheritance. I will praise the Lord, who counsels me; even at night my heart instructs me. I keep my eyes always on the Lord. With him at my right hand, I will not be shaken."

The reference to boundary lines was about as clear of an acknowledgment to proceed with radiation as we could have ever imagined. A calming presence then came over Tina, and she felt such peace knowing God was in control. As a result of God's leading to proceed with radiation, Tina gave the thumbs-up to begin. The treatments involved receiving targeted radiation to her chest area over a span of 28 days. She endured the daily radiation but seemed to lose some energy as the treatments progressed. By the end of the 28 days, her skin was quite red in the area that had been radiated for nearly a month. The procedure was considered successful by the radiation oncologist, if for no other reason than it was a proactive step in preventing any cancer cell migration.

Once again, the Lord had provided clear instruction, and Tina had followed His directive.

8

Discovering New Spiritual Pathways

In the years that followed Tina's first round of chemo and radiation, she became involved with a women's Bible study and prayer group that met weekly on Monday evenings on the southwest side of town. She really enjoyed her fellowship with these ladies. They were predominantly older women, and most of them went to different churches in the East Texas area or participated in home church groups. Some were married, some were divorced or widowed, and some were single. They came from different socioeconomic backgrounds and had different life experiences. However, they all had one thing in common—an intense zeal for the Lord. Tina typically referred to them as prayer warriors as they devoted a significant amount of their meeting time to prayer.

Tina asked me to go with her to one of the meetings in the summer of 2000. I must admit I was a bit apprehensive about attending the meeting, but at Tina's urging, I decided to go. As we entered the building that night, calming music was playing in the background, and several people were already in prayer. We were told the activities for that night would be devoted to intercessory prayer followed by some words from a traveling pastor at the end of the evening.

It was not long before I sensed the passion, depth, and sincerity of these prayer warriors. Some could speak in tongues, some would lie on the floor or in unique positions while praying, some would cry out to the Lord in the middle of a silent prayer, and some would pray for up to an hour at a time without ever moving. However, what was most noteworthy to me was that the physical appearance of these ladies seemed to change as they prayed. It seemed as if they were being filled with spiritual energy that manifested itself as a physical change to their bodies. Although I couldn't explain it, there was definitely a difference in their facial appearances and skin tones immediately before and after the prayer session. When I mentioned this to Tina, she just smiled and said, "God is responsible for that." I would learn in subsequent years that the changes in skin tone and body temperature, and the presence of materials such as "gold dust" on the bodies of prayer intercessors, were actually quite common after intense prayer sessions.

As Tina and I drove home after the meeting, we talked about what had transpired that night. It was easy to see why she enjoyed these meetings so much. She was being spiritually fed and mentored by older women of the faith. Not only did they pray over her and give her renewed strength and courage, but they also imparted wisdom and knowledge to her, much in the same manner as the prayer warriors that came to her parents' home when she was first diagnosed with cancer. Indeed, Tina was seeking physical, mental, and spiritual energy from the Lord with the help of these ladies.

It was not surprising that Tina bonded with them and developed lasting friendships. Their collective yearning for the Lord simply transcended everything else. They often spoke of doing battle in the spiritual realm when they gathered. In fact, many of their Bible studies and prayers focused on the theme of equipping yourself to conduct spiritual warfare. Although this topic was relatively new to me, the concept of fighting Satan during trials and tribulations certainly made sense. I learned that spiritual warfare was more than equipping yourself with the armor of God as outlined in Ephesians 6 in the Bible. It also meant we are to actively pray against the devil and all the spiritual forces of evil in this world. These forces are ever-present and all around us.

I am glad that Tina befriended these ladies and became part of their prayer group. She benefited from a deeper understanding of God's Word through these relationships. I must admit that a lot of the spiritual passion and vision she received from these prayer warriors rubbed off on me. I began to look at things through a different lens. Tina and I would need all this new spiritual vision and courage to fight another battle. It seemed her medical condition was about to change again.

9

It's Back

In October 2004, Tina's oncologist in Tyler reported that the tumor markers in her blood had significantly increased during her latest battery of tests. She also reported that a positron emission tomography (PET) scan revealed a tumor in the sternum-chest area, as well as two lesions on her liver. Needless to say, we were blindsided by the news since Tina had been in remission for more than five years and was now considered in the same cancer risk pool as the general female population. After giving us a few minutes to digest the unsettling news, the oncologist said she would be happy to show us the films if we wanted to view them. Tina did not want to examine the films for obvious reasons. After all, who could possibly concentrate on looking at medical information when you have just been told the two words no cancer patient in remission wants to hear—*it's back!* Sensing Tina might have problems communicating any further thoughts, I asked the doctor what her suggested path forward was based on the new information. She relayed three possible regimens for chemotherapy.

At this point, I knew Tina wanted to take her cancer treatment elsewhere. She had never really bonded with the local oncologist, and honestly, the oncologist didn't have a bedside manner that was encouraging to someone fighting cancer. She always seemed distant and relayed important information in an impersonal manner. She never acknowledged the importance of mental and spiritual fitness and the impact it can have on a cancer patient. She also seemed perturbed that the oncologist in Houston was always copied on all documentation and test results. Before I could say anything, Tina told the oncologist that her clinic was no longer the place for her follow-up care. Tina then went on to say that she had a really big God and would return to Houston to get another opinion. As we walked out of the oncologist's office that day, we realized that another chapter was unfolding in our lives. Once again, we sought the Lord for our next steps.

Tina committed the next few days to intense prayer and inquired of the Lord for a clear path forward. She received these words of encouragement: "Do not let your hearts be troubled. You believe in God; believe also in me" (John 14:1). These words reminded her that we are not to fear but to abide in Christ, and He will be our peace. We then prayed together that God would give revelation knowledge to Tina's situation and shine the light of truth on her circumstance.

We met with Tina's oncologist in Houston, and he recommended trying three months of an estrogen-blocking drug followed by another drug used in breast cancer patients with hormone-receptor-positive tumors. He was hopeful that this approach would work in lieu of going the chemo route. We followed his guidance, and Tina used the prescribed medications for three months. Unfortunately, lab results revealed that the two-drug therapy did not provide a favorable response. As a result, the oncologist recommended moving on to chemotherapy in January 2005. The thought of enduring another regimen of chemo was certainly not pleasant for either of us. However, Tina embraced the new cancer treatment plan and was determined to make the best of it.

After one round of the new chemo program, we decided the rigors of frequent trips to Houston for treatments would take an unnecessary toll on Tina and me. It seemed God was now pointing us back to Tyler for future cancer treatment. We spent a considerable amount of time in prayer, asking God to lead us to a new, local oncologist who could shepherd Tina's cancer journey from here forward. The next day, I mentioned at my office that Tina and I were seeking a new oncologist. Unbeknownst to me, I had a colleague whose wife worked at an oncology clinic in Tyler. It was different than the one we had used. My colleague raved about an oncologist at the clinic who was quickly earning a reputation as one of the most caring and respected doctors in the East Texas area. After receiving the heads-up regarding this cancer specialist, we inquired of several people, including nurses, doctors, and patients, who had a working knowledge of this physician. Without exception, all feedback we received was extremely positive. Tina was equally impressed with this doctor based on television interviews she had seen and what she had read about her in magazine articles and newspapers. She was also pleased to learn that this oncologist treats the whole human being (body, mind, and spirit), not just the disease. In addition, Tina learned that she was a real champion for women and frequently participated in breast cancer fundraising events and other activities promoting women's health. As such, we hired the new oncologist.

During the first office visit with the new doctor, we talked about Tina's medical condition and cancer journey and how

God had led her to this moment in time. The physician spent a considerable amount of time conveying hope and using positive language to convey a path forward. It was obvious that she was passionate about helping people get to a better place. Her methodology of treating the whole person, including the spirit, was evident when she spoke. She had an energizing personality similar to Tina's, so it was easy to see that Tina was going to bond with her. At the end of our consultation, which lasted nearly an hour, I asked the doctor if I could pray over her. She welcomed the invitation, and we all held hands.

As we left the clinic that day, I didn't have to ask Tina if she was comfortable with the new doctor. That was a no-brainer. God had already made that decision for us when He led us to her. Tina simply smiled and responded to my silent question, "Yes, we are in the right place."

10

Round Two

When the new oncologist took over Tina's case, she added another chemotherapy drug to the treatment plan. This drug immediately had a positive therapeutic impact, and the tumor markers quickly declined. However, the addition of the new drug also had some serious side effects. Tina's hands were literally burnt after just a few treatments and her hands and feet became severely swollen. These undesirable side effects were also accompanied by complete hair loss and loss of fingernails and toenails. I must admit the loss of protective coverings on the fingers and toes was hard to digest. Nonetheless, Tina learned to put "bag balm" on her hands and feet to provide some soothing relief and then covered them with cotton gloves and footies. Tina also recommissioned her fashionable headwear to address the hair loss. During all of this, including the usual energy loss and heightened risk of infection, Tina remained vigilant and committed to the treatment program. She never complained about having to wear coverings on her head, hands, and feet. Her current situation in life also prohibited her from doing most normal activities. To say the least, it was not a pleasant time for her.

Tina's commitment to see the treatment program through to the end despite all the side effects paid off. Six months after starting chemotherapy regimen number two, the tumor markers were back in the normal range. As a result of her successful response to the chemo, the doctor lifted Tina's travel restriction, and our family was able to take a well-deserved vacation to Colorado. It provided a retreat for Tina who left behind the monotony of everyday life and medical regimens. She was able to relax and enjoy the mountains and beautiful outdoors. She welcomed the opportunity to ride bikes with her family, even at elevations as high as 6,000 feet. God must have given her an infusion of energy since she was able to keep pace with the boys and me as we rode up steep inclines. Several times during the bike rides and accompanying walks in the woods, we just stopped to pray and thank God for His presence in our lives and for directing Tina's cancer journey. God's beautiful creation has a way of making you feel closer to Him, so it was totally natural to thank our Heavenly Father in

the midst of such beauty. I am convinced that the Colorado trip was part of God's divine therapy for Tina at this point of her life. The exercise was extremely beneficial, especially after having her hands and feet in wrappings for an extended period.

Not long after the vacation, the rigors of life with chemotherapy came back. Tina continued an oral drug program until her scans worsened in 2005. When it became apparent the oral approach was providing minimal therapeutic benefits, Tina had to revert to more traditional infusion drugs for the remainder of the year. At the beginning of 2006, yet another menu of chemotherapy drugs entered her life. Tina and I wrestled with two clinical trial choices that were presented to us. Once again, we inquired of the Lord. "Call to me and I will answer you and tell you great and unsearchable things you do not know" (Jer. 33:3). We asked for supernatural wisdom for the oncologist and another doctor Tina had asked the oncologist to consult with. After much prayer and discussion, we all agreed on a clinical trial program that would begin immediately.

By now the oncologist knew that Tina's faith was strong and that she relied on God to give her answers and guidance. Sensing a spiritual connection, the doctor introduced Tina to another cancer survivor. They quickly became spiritual buddies and began working on an inaugural breast cancer survivor retreat in February 2006. After one of the work sessions, Tina and her new friend decided to go pray at her friend's church. Tina had been seeking God's input through prayer but confided she was not receiving clear communication from her Heavenly Father on the major health issues she was now facing. Tina prayed specifically for a message regarding her condition so she would not misunderstand. She prayed, "Lord, I don't care if you have to send me a letter or call me on the telephone, just speak clearly."

Arriving home after her in-depth prayer session, Tina retrieved the mail from the mailbox. In it was a small package from a woman she barely knew and someone who didn't know her personal situation. In the package was a short note that said, "Tina, I understand you have some health problems, and I thought this might encourage you." Inside the box was a mustard seed necklace with a portion of Scripture from Matthew 17:20 inscribed on the back: "*If you have the faith of a mustard seed . . .*" Tina immediately fell to her knees and exclaimed, "Father, forgive me for doubting You. Thank You for giving me Your message through Your chosen servant. It will serve as a constant reminder regarding faith and placing my trust in You. I will cherish it always."

The same week Tina received the mustard seed necklace, her good friend Cody was visiting Colorado. Cody was also a cancer survivor and frankly was a walking miracle due to the number of times she had been told she probably wouldn't live much longer. Cody called to check on Tina and inquired in regard to the progress of her latest chemotherapy program. Tina informed Cody that she was going to start a clinical trial and that she needed her prayers before she started the new experimental treatment. After they visited on the phone for a while, Tina told Cody, "Go see something fabulous, and when you see it, say a prayer for me." That evening Cody called Tina and said, "Tina, you won't believe it. We were coming out of a restaurant tonight in Colorado, and there in the sky was a double rainbow. I knew it was just for you." Cody had never seen a double rainbow before but knew of the importance of rainbows on Tina's faith journey. She was simply overwhelmed by the colorful panoramic display. Upon hearing of the double rainbow, Tina exclaimed, "Now God is speaking with rainbows through my friends!"

11

Visited by an Angel

Tina developed a mouth sore in early 2006 after only one round of the clinical trial drugs. She promptly got it evaluated, and it was determined to be cancerous. The cancer cells in Tina's mouth turned out to be different than the breast cancer cells, according to the pathology results. Since the oral cancer was a new type of cancer, Tina was removed from the clinical trial program. She now had to pursue a path that addressed two different types of cancer without the support of the newly developed research drugs.

A computed tomography (CT) scan of the mouth and neck was performed shortly after the oral cancer was discovered. The good news was that the lymph nodes in the neck and chest region were clear. However, the CT scan revealed some troublesome lesions in the brain. Tina's oncologist immediately ordered a magnetic resonance imaging (MRI) scan of her brain, and the unsettling procedure was performed the following day. The MRI indicated there was something in her brain that was not supposed to be there. However, the images of the problematic areas didn't look like a typical progression of breast cancer. The medical staff considered other possibilities for the origin of the lesions. However, other cancer-development scenarios didn't make much sense because Tina was asymptomatic in regard to this new finding. It was also puzzling to her oncologist that the lesions were discovered by accident.

Tina's oncologist was visibly shaken over this new discovery. Tina sensed the doctor's disillusionment and told her that she has a "big, big God." She said, "I know my God would not have revealed this situation in my brain if He did not want us to have knowledge of it and to do something about it." As much as I was reeling from the disheartening news myself, I had to admire the spirit of my wife for staying positive during this evolving, chaotic situation.

Tina and I were quickly put in touch with a distinguished brain surgeon in Tyler who reviewed the CT scans and MRI of the brain. He acknowledged the presence of the cancerous areas and indicated that surgery would need to be performed to address the problematic lesions. Together, we agreed that we needed to determine the exact cell type of the lesions to properly evaluate post-surgical treatment options. The surgeon recommended an open brain biopsy to accomplish this. He carefully explained the details of the surgery and answered all our questions about this delicate procedure. As the surgeon talked about cranial details and other intricate issues involving brain matter, I tried to digest how fast things were moving in regard to diagnoses and procedures. It seemed just a few days ago we were talking about promising research drugs to combat breast cancer, and now we were discussing brain surgery to address another type of cancer in Tina's body. Although the breadth of thought was a bit overwhelming, I was thankful that actions were being taken in a prudent and expeditious manner to maximize the chances for a successful outcome.

Tina and I spent a significant amount of time on our knees as we prepared for her brain surgery. Prayer warriors also came to the house and covered her in prayer. Out-of-town family and friends scheduled trips to Tyler and provided food and housekeeping services to address the never-ending chores of feeding a family and maintaining a home. The outpouring of support was indeed a blessing and yet another example of how God provided physical, emotional, and spiritual support to our family.

The following week, Tina was admitted to the hospital in preparation for the brain surgery. The morning before the surgery, we asked the Lord to give us a sign that we were in the right place. Upon arriving at the hospital, we learned that the receptionist's name at the check-in desk was Grace and that the surgery coordinator's name was Jay Beth (similar to Jabez in the Bible). Jay Beth gave Tina prayer beads. If that were not enough, the receptionist's name in the surgical waiting area was Angel. *Okay, Lord. Message received again. We are in the right place!*

After all the admittance paperwork was completed, we met with the brain surgeon for a consultation and the required pre-op procedures. The surgeon shaved Tina's head and made preliminary markings on her cranium in preparation for the surgery. He then prayed with us. We took the opportunity to pray for him also and thank him for his God-given abilities and his calling to help people with serious medical issues. He told us that God had gifted him with his surgical skills and emphasized that the successful brain surgeries were not of him but of God and that God just uses his hands. He then went over the surgical risks and advised us that since the lesions to be biopsied were on the left side of the brain with the language center, it could affect Tina's ability to speak afterward. Tina sensed the potential language disruption was an attempt by Satan to shut down her testimony regarding Christ and what the Lord had already done for her. She told the surgeon that God was in charge of her speaking capabilities and He would not let the evil one silence her. She proclaimed that God was using her to tell His story. At this moment, I was ready to stand up and cheer for my wife. She had just been told that she may never speak again or possibly suffer reduced language skills. Yet here she was proclaiming the gospel and that God was in control!

After we finished the presurgery preparations with the brain surgeon, Tina had CT scans and an MRI to provide needed baseline data. All the necessary testing was completed by 10:30 that morning. Due to the early completion, Tina was able to check in to her hospital room and get some rest before lunch. Since we had the rest of the day free, Tina and I took the opportunity after lunch to spend time in prayer and worship and praise the Lord. We firmly knew that God would see us through this difficult situation. After our prayer time, we roamed around the hospital to get some exercise and have a change of scenery from the confines of the hospital room. Along the way, we saw a distressed lady in the radiology waiting room who apparently was waiting to get a CT scan. Tina, without hesitation, advised me to go over and pray for that lady. I followed her directive and prayed over the woman who was obviously nervous about her pending situation. I distinctly remember her looking up at me and saying, "I was just waiting for someone to pray for me." I told her that God had heard her prayer request and simply used Tina and me to be her intercessors.

Tina and I then proceeded to the patio garden on the fourth floor of the hospital. It was our intent to pray and take personal communion in this serene location. The garden was full of greenery and provided a place for quiet meditation and reflection. We chose a table and two chairs in a secluded part of the garden. As we sat down and prepared to take communion, we took a deep breath, and immediately a distinct smell came between the two of us. It was the sweet smell of roses. However, there were no roses in the garden. I asked Tina, "Did you smell that?" and she answered yes. I then asked, "Does it smell like roses to you?" Once again, Tina said yes. She followed this response with "Jesus is here, and He is revealing Himself to us." She then cited the familiar verse from Song of Solomon 2:1: "I am a rose of Sharon, a lily of the valleys." Tina said she had received the rose smell previously at a local eatery where she and another prayer warrior had met for lunch. She also relayed stories of other believers she had met who had experienced the sweet rose fragrance. She now proclaimed that the Lord was revealing His presence to both of us as we were about to honor Him in communion. Needless to say, the presence of the rose smell boosted our faith at that moment. It seemed God had sent the Holy Spirit to communicate with us in a unique way prior to Tina's brain surgery.

After we finished communion, we went back to the hospital room. Tina felt led to study John 15:15: "I no longer call you servants, because a servant does not know his master's business. Instead, I have called you friends, for everything that I learned from my Father I have made known to you." After that, she randomly flipped some pages in her Bible and read aloud 3 John 2–4: "Dear friend, I pray that you may enjoy good health and that all may go well with you, even as your soul is getting along well. It gave me great joy when some believers came and testified about your faithfulness to the truth, telling how you continue to walk in it. I have no greater joy than to hear that my children are walking in the truth." Tina wept as she looked up at me after reading those verses. She was simply overwhelmed by the repeated citations of God's faithfulness to her.

After Tina finished the Bible readings, she lay down on the hospital bed and began praising God with her arms lifted high. She was simply in a euphoric state after being called "friend" by Jesus Christ. After praising the Lord, she prayed for angels to surround the hospital room with their swords drawn to protect her. She then inquired of her Savior, "Lord, what does all this mean? What do you want me to do?" As she continued praying, Tina said she could feel "electricity" on her tongue. She remarked that this bioelectrical phenomenon was a strange sensation unlike any she had ever felt before. She said she could sense the Holy Spirit filling her body as she received this unique electrical stimulation. The electricity was like a sizzle when she spoke. I must admit her words seemed to possess a new level of clarity during this excited state. She recited several Bible verses during the minutes that followed and then indicated that God had revealed another directive for her. "He told me to speak to the nations," she said. However, she confided that she didn't understand what He meant. I simply replied that God would reveal the answer to that mystery in due time.

At that point, it was apparent that Tina was exhausted from the day's activities, and she fell asleep. I pulled up a chair and propped my feet on her bed, sensing this was a good time to also get some rest. After a short while, Tina suddenly awoke from her nap and started singing over and over, "Alleluia, alleluia, alleluia." While she was singing, my eyes remained closed as I reclined in the chair in a semiconscious state. Suddenly, the tone of her singing voice changed to a very high pitch with much vibrato. I opened my eyes and asked if someone had entered the room singing. Tina said, "No, I was singing." I quipped, "No, that was not your voice. I know what your voice sounds like, and that definitely was not yours." To this day, I am still not sure of the origin of that voice. All I know is that it was not Tina's. She always believed that angels took over her voice and praised God with beautiful sounds as she worshipped Him from the hospital bed.

The afternoon quickly gave way to evening. We had agreed to meet with family and friends in the main hospital lobby so that all who came could extend their thoughts and prayers to Tina. Andrew, our oldest son, played several songs on his guitar, and many in our support group joined in to sing some familiar praise and worship songs. Many other visitors who were in nearby waiting areas also joined in the choral refrains to celebrate their faith. After Andrew finished playing, Tina started "preaching" to those gathered and recited some of the special moments she and I had experienced earlier in the day. It was a moment in time that I will never forget as she told those who had gathered that the blood of the Lamb was slain for all of us so we might have eternal life with Him. She then spoke of God's love for us and how He would never leave us or forsake us. At the end of her message, we had a large prayer circle, and each person had a chance to pray over Tina.

After the prayers, all the people who had gathered to support Tina said their goodbyes and left the hospital. Finally, only Tina and I remained. However, as we were turning to leave the lobby, we noticed an older woman sitting in a chair in the waiting area adjacent to the sitting area we were in. She immediately jumped up when we noticed her, pointed right at Tina, and exclaimed, "You speak the truth!" There was a distinct glow around this person who appeared to be in her late 50s or 60s by human standards. She was by herself, wore a hat, and had olive-colored skin.

For the next 45 minutes, I witnessed a verbal exchange between Tina and this "person" who could only be described as heavenly. The angelic being spoke with such authority and proclaimed, "It's all about the blood!" Tina glorified God's mighty healing power and His awesome majesty. She proclaimed God's providence as revealed to her through Scripture, prayer, and, most notably, the human senses of sight, sound, and smell. A spiritual fog seemed to engulf the waiting area as the two females exchanged exhortations. Both had gold dust covering their bodies as they praised the Lord and recited the need for God's people to rise up and claim victory in Jesus. Finally, the unknown lady, who never mentioned her name or why she was at the hospital, exclaimed, "My God, my God, that's enough. It's just enough." She then pointed her finger at Tina and boldly proclaimed, "You will speak to the nations!" Then, without fanfare, she got up and left. No one came to pick her up as she quietly exited the front doors of the hospital.

I looked at Tina whose face was still glowing as if she just had a heavenly encounter. Her skin still had gold dust on it. Make no mistake, her physical appearance was different than before the encounter. I quickly walked over to the front desk in the lobby (only 15–20 feet away from where we had been sitting) and asked the security person on duty if he saw where the older woman went. His response was, "What woman?" I then raced out the front doors to see if I could get another glimpse of this heavenly creature. It was easy to see in all directions since the front visitor parking lot was basically empty due to the late hour (now about midnight). I scanned all directions and could not see any person. I went back in the hospital and looked around just to make sure she was not inside the lobby in some remote area. I even checked the bathrooms, but there was no trace of her anywhere.

I went back to the waiting area, and before I could say anything, Tina said, "Did you see the angel again?" She always had a way of cutting right to the heart of spiritual matters. "No," I replied. "She is gone." Tina just nodded. We then went back to her hospital room. The hospital staff was wondering where we had been for so many hours. Tina and I talked about the heavenly encounter that had just occurred in the lobby. Interestingly, Tina thought the encounter with the angel had lasted only a few minutes. She had no comprehension that the exchange had lasted much longer and that the appearance of her and the other "person" had changed during the discussion.

After relaying the story of the angelic encounter, Tina asked the nurse assigned to her room for an extra pillow. The nurse replied, "Oh, those are scarce around here, especially on the oncology floor." She then went next door and found two extra pillows in that room and one extra pillow in Tina's closet. She said, "Oh my gosh! This never happens. We never have extra pillows!" Tina just smiled and said, "God knows what we need when we need it." She then started testifying to the nurse about all that God had done for her that day, including the rose smell, Scripture confirmations of God's protection over her health, and "speaking to the nations." Despite all the heavenly encounters and spiritual signs, the nurse remained skeptical about Tina's testimony.

After Tina and I talked for another 10 minutes about the day's events, an attendant came into the room to take Tina's vital signs. We learned that this person was a retired pastor who spent his nonworking hours sending sermons, testimonies, and other spiritual information to third-world countries via shortwave radio. He was supposed to have had the night off, but somebody had called in sick, and he was asked to fill in. (Imagine that!) The man listened intently as Tina retold her story regarding the day's activities. After he left, I told Tina, "That is how you will speak to the nations! God will use him to send your testimony to people around the world!" Just as I finished speaking, the gentleman walked back in and said, "Mrs. Heimbaugh, would you mind recording your story on a CD? I will make sure it gets sent to people who need to hear it." He then left the room and continued his rounds. I looked over at Tina and said, "There you go. God has spoken!" Tina's nurse, who was still in the room and had witnessed all of this, exclaimed, "That's it. I am getting my Bible out and will start reading it again." No longer could she deny God's handiwork in all these special moments.

Tina did go on to "speak to the nations" many times. Looking back on that evening, God had used a heavenly encounter with an angel to proclaim His glory through His servant on earth.

12

Energized by His Spirit

More confirmations regarding Tina's health were revealed the morning of Tina's brain surgery. The oncologist dropped by Tina's hospital room to check on her. She said she had called the brain surgeon early in the morning to inquire about the risks associated with Tina's brain biopsy. While they were discussing the delicate procedure and as the oncologist was backing out of her driveway, she saw a rainbow in the misty air from her sprinkler system. She immediately interrupted their medical discussion and said, "I just saw a rainbow. Everything will be fine with Tina."

After hearing that, Tina showed her a picture she had received the day before of a double rainbow her friend had seen while vacationing in Colorado. It was encased in a green frame with the words "I found joy in a big God." The doctor just shook her head and exclaimed, "There are rainbows everywhere."

At last, the time came for the brain biopsy procedure. I must say that of all the surgical procedures I have personally endured or have had close friends or relatives experience, any procedure that involves drilling into the skull is the most unnerving. We covered Tina in prayer prior to the surgery. Several people came and sat with me in the surgical waiting area, sensing I needed support due to the gravity of the situation. Yet despite the scariness of a cranial procedure and the potential side effects associated with it, a calming presence came over me. Perhaps it was the peace referenced in Philippians 4:7: "And the peace of God, which transcends all understanding, will guard your hearts and your minds in Christ Jesus." I knew God was in control and that Tina would survive the procedure with minimal speech impediment.

After the multi-hour procedure was completed, I was able to see Tina and pray over her. She was drowsy from all the medications but was awake enough to acknowledge my presence. Her new shaved look and head bandages did not alarm me one bit. I was just glad to see her and tell her I loved her. The brain surgeon told me Tina had endured the procedure well but reminded me of the possible speech issues that could follow. I told him I was not worried about that. My wife was more than capable of communicating her thoughts and spiritual messages via nonverbal methods, if needed. The doctor, who seldom smiled due to his unemotional disposition, managed to crack a smile in response.

In the days that followed Tina's brain biopsy, the focus shifted to follow-up treatment for the brain cancer, which was taking priority over everything else going on in Tina's body. The pathology results from the biopsy samples indicated that the lesions were the same type as the breast cancer cells. Therefore, a single chemotherapy program could be constructed to treat all the unwanted cancer cells, regardless of their location. However, the prevailing opinion from the medical community was that radiation needed to be performed on Tina's brain as soon as possible before any systemic drug regimen was implemented.

At face value, radiating the head seemed like something that would cause more harm than good. However, the brain surgeon and oncology folks were firm in their recommendation regarding radiation as the best path forward to address the brain cancer. Once again, Tina and I inquired of the Lord as to what to do. We also requested that our prayer warriors pray fervently regarding brain radiation. Tina advised the medical staff, family, and friends that she must wait on the Lord to provide His plan for her before she would allow treatment of any kind, including radiation.

The night before the scheduled brain radiation consultation, Tina and I were lying in bed, mentally preparing for the next day's activities. I asked if she had gotten any word yet from the Lord regarding radiation. She said, "Not yet." Then she replied, "It may be 11:59 p.m., but He will answer my prayer and tell me what to do." She then picked up a book she had been reading earlier in the day called *Out of the Wilderness: My Healing Journey through Cancer and Cancerous Lies*, a journal by Jean Shen. Tina began reading where she had previously left off. Interestingly, the part of the book Tina was about to read depicted a conversation between God and the author. In response to the author's health situation, God said, "You are worrying about the cancer treatment? No need to fret. I will send the right people to help you navigate through the maze. It will be voices you can trust. Do not be troubled." Tina promptly closed the book after reading these sentences and dropped to her knees. She praised the Lord for the message she needed to hear. The time was 12:02 a.m. It seemed God had answered Tina's prayer just three minutes after her proclamation to wait on the Lord for an answer.

That night, Tina and I slept like babies. God removed any anxiety we felt over the pending radiation treatment and provided our bodies with much-needed rest. We arrived at the radiation treatment center the next morning, fully refreshed and optimistic. We were anxious to see more confirmations of God's hand in Tina's cancer treatment. We were also seeking validation of the treatment location. Lo and behold, we received two distinct signs from God that we were in the right place. At the check-in desk, we noticed the name of the patient who signed in just ahead of Tina—Lily Majestic Ross. The word *majestic* quickly caught Tina's attention since God had been speaking to her using this word during her recent prayer time. Tina quipped, "How many people sign in using their full name, let alone have the name Majestic?" Tina also focused on Lily, the first name. She knew the lily is considered the most significant flower for Christians and is a symbol for purity. She also knew the fragrant flower is a representation of Jesus's resurrection. After scrutinizing the registration logbook for a few minutes, Tina exclaimed, "Lily Majestic is a sign from God."

After we finished postulating over the significance of Lily Majestic Ross and why this person just happened to be there on the same day as Tina, we made our way to the radiation clinic waiting area. As we turned to sit down in the waiting room, we noticed a huge picture of a rainbow on the wall. *Okay, Lord. Message received again. We are in the right place!* The picture was actually a puzzle of Noah's Ark with a rainbow above it. The puzzle had been put together by cancer patients. Tina screamed with excitement as she observed it on the wall. God had spoken to her yet again through a unique rainbow. If there was any doubt in our minds whether radiation was the correct therapy for Tina or whether this clinic was the correct administrator of the treatment, God just removed all doubt. Not only had He provided a rainbow picture on a wall to confirm the location, but He had also provided key words in a logbook to confirm His presence and His plan. I guess God decided that due to the complexity of Tina's health situation, we needed not one sign from Him *but two*!

As we sat down in the waiting area, Tina saw her oncologist down the hallway and waved to her. The doctor came over, and Tina quickly pointed out the rainbow on the wall. Of course, her oncologist was well aware of the significance of rainbows in Tina's cancer journey and the spiritual impact they had on her. When she saw the picture that apparently had been placed on the wall just a few days prior to our appointment, she gasped. She then turned to the other patients in the waiting area and told them to listen to Tina's rainbow stories as a source of encouragement. Many of those waiting for their scheduled treatments listened to some of the "rainbow moments" Tina shared. At this point, I wondered silently, *Is Tina here for brain radiation treatment or is God simply using her as a mouthpiece to minister to cancer patients?* I quickly concluded that both objectives were worthy and needed to be fulfilled. After all, God had just provided two confirmations of His presence. When the receptionist said they were running slightly behind schedule that morning, I just smiled. God was giving Tina time to tell His story to a roomful of people who needed some encouragement. Due to the slight delay in the schedule, Tina was able to share a few special spiritual moments from her cancer journey with the other patients. After she finished her second rainbow story, she was summoned for her initial consultation and placement of head markings.

The next day, we arrived promptly at 9:30 a.m. for Tina's first radiation treatment. The treatment was completed quickly and without difficulty. Upon exiting the treatment room, Tina's oncology nurse was waiting for her. She said, "This is for you." It was a glass craft marble that had fallen off a cabinet in the oncologist's office and onto the doctor's toe as she passed by the cabinet. The marble-drop event occurred precisely at 9:30 a.m. The oncologist knew that Tina's first brain radiation treatment was at 9:30 that morning, so she understood the significance of the time associated with this unusual event. The marble drop apparently gave her confidence and confirmation that Tina was indeed following God's plan. Upon receiving the special marble, Tina relayed to the nurse that the oncologist should read Isaiah 43:10: "'You are my witnesses,' declares the LORD, 'and my servant whom I have chosen, so that you may know and believe me and understand that I am he.'"

The brain radiation treatments were scheduled every day for 10 days. However, as the treatments progressed, Tina's mouth began to hurt severely from sores that were developing on her jaw and tongue. We made the decision to let the doctors promptly go ahead and remove the jaw cancer and a large portion of the left side of her tongue. The mouth surgery was supposed to be an outpatient procedure but turned into a four-night hospital stay. The good news was that the oral surgeon successfully removed the tumor and got clear margins in the areas around the excised tongue. On the downside, the surgeon had to remove more of the tongue than initially planned in order to completely remove the tumor. As a result, we were told that Tina may not speak clearly ever again.

As Tina recuperated in the hospital from the combined effects of the brain radiation and oral surgery, the Lord gave her a Scripture He had given her exactly 10 years earlier.

Then your light will break forth like the dawn,
and your healing will quickly appear;
then your righteousness will go before you,
and the glory of the LORD will be your rear guard.
Then you will call, and the LORD will answer;
you will cry for help, and he will say: Here am I.

—Isa. 58:8–9

Tina's oncologist came to check on her during her unplanned hospital stay and inquired how she felt. Tina responded by singing, "Alleluia." Her doctor was surprised with the unexpected vocal capability. Tina just smiled and said, "I have a big God." Tina was also advised in the days that followed that she may never have hair again due to the brain radiation. To the amazement of her doctors, she grew back a full head of hair after the radiation treatments were completed.

Yes, the Lord was Tina's rear guard during this fragile time in her life. He provided the necessary life-giving energy that others simply could not understand. The medical community had predicted reduced physical, mental, and vocal capabilities due to the intense procedures Tina had endured. However, it seemed God had other plans for her. He provided healing beyond explanation due to His infusion of spiritual energy to Tina's head and mouth. Alleluia, indeed!

13

Not Today, Satan!

Tina had committed to speaking at an American Cancer Society (ACS) fundraiser in Dallas scheduled in August 2006. One of the members of the organizing committee had heard of Tina's speaking abilities and infectious passion and thought she would make an excellent motivational speaker for the event. She had contacted Tina earlier in the year (before her brain and mouth surgeries) regarding her potential participation. But now, due to Tina's weakened state after her multiple surgeries and follow-up treatment during the summer of 2006, I questioned whether it was still a good idea for her to speak at the fundraiser. I reminded Tina that the doctors had cautioned her about the chance of seizures and the risk of falling due to balance issues, which were both elevated after her brain surgery. Although she was currently taking medication to minimize potential seizures, the doctors advised her against participating in any events outside the home or any activities requiring significant physical exertion. I should have known that my query regarding Tina's decision to speak at the event was not what my wife wanted to hear. Her energizer personality and perseverance to see things through were simply not going to let her pass up this opportunity. She simply responded, "God has orchestrated this event. If He did not want me to speak, He would have silenced my voice. I must go and proclaim His goodness."

Given Tina's determination to speak at the fundraiser, we spent the week leading up to the event preparing a rough outline of her remarks. I thought it was important for Tina to keep notes in front of her during her speech in case her mind wandered and she got off track. After hours of discussion over a general theme and specific topics, we finalized the content and did a few practice runs to ensure the message was not too long. We were advised that her message should be limited to 20 minutes.

In order to provide Tina with as much rest as possible before the event, we drove to Dallas the day before and stayed at the hotel where the ACS fundraiser was being held. That way Tina could sleep for a few extra hours in the morning. The fundraiser was the same weekend our oldest son was scheduled to move in to his dormitory for his freshman year at the University of North Texas. As such, we decided to combine both activities and make a weekend of it. Tina's parents and sister also made the trip. Her mom and sister were registered for the fundraising event, and her dad was there for support. Andrew and Grant also made the trip to support their mother. Thus, our caravan to Dallas included seven people, three cars, one trailer containing college stuff, and suitcases full of fancy women's clothes and hats.

At last the time came for the start of the fundraiser. It was being held in a conference room and lobby of a hotel near the Dallas/Fort Worth International Airport. The event was a high tea luncheon combined with a live, silent auction. Attendance was limited to females. Participants were largely from the Dallas area, but there were also women from other cities around the country. All the attendees were dressed up in colorful, tea-sipping outfits and stylish hats.

Since the fundraiser was a women-only event, all males, including myself, my father-in-law, and my sons, were not allowed inside the conference room for the luncheon. However, event organizers said we could stand at the back of the room during Tina's talk. I was glad to be allowed access to the room since I was very nervous about Tina's physical condition. The podium where she would speak required her to take a large step onto the top platform. I was unsure if she would be able to navigate that step and wanted to be close by in case she needed assistance or if she fell and seriously injured herself.

The luncheon featured two speakers—a widely regarded breast surgeon from the Dallas area and Tina. The surgeon provided an update on breast cancer treatments and research and development efforts. She spoke in a very professional tone and relayed that advances were being made on several fronts. Although the tone of her talk was positive, it was obvious that talk of cancer treatment was uncomfortable for many of the fundraiser attendees.

As the doctor finished her remarks, Tina was summoned to the platform. I stood at the back of the room, ready to move in case Tina needed help. However, God had His hand on her as she climbed the difficult step with minimal effort. Once on top of the platform, Tina looked out over the sea of people at the luncheon. She smiled, grabbed the microphone, and began talking. Fewer than two minutes into her talk, she was already off script. It was obvious that she didn't need any notes and that God was going to give her the words to speak to this group of women who needed to hear an uplifting story.

She began speaking with conviction and relayed her story of initially being brushed off and misdiagnosed. She then focused on how God spoke to her through rainbows and other signs to develop a path forward regarding her cancer journey. As Tina spoke, I looked around the room, and every woman at each table was listening intently to Tina's words. As she described several of her "God moments," she seemed to connect with each attendee on an emotional level. They were obviously in need of encouragement, and Tina's message was hitting home. By the time Tina got to the part of her story about the angelic visit the evening before her brain surgery, people were hanging on her every word. Again, I scanned the room, and to my surprise, the back of the conference room was now filled with hotel employees and other support staff. Apparently, the message had passed around the hotel to all employees that they needed to come to the conference room immediately and hear this lady's story. Standing room only now took on a whole new meaning.

Tina's message reached a crescendo when she got to the part about her tongue surgery. She told the crowd that doctors said she may never talk again or, at the very least, would have slurred speech. Then, without hesitation, she exclaimed, "The devil may cut out my tongue and try to stop me from talking, but I will never stop proclaiming the good news of Jesus and what He has done for me!" The attendees erupted instantaneously with cheers, whistles, amens, and other verbal confirmations. It was the most electric and spontaneous moment I had ever witnessed in my life. Just minutes before, the vast majority of these people didn't know one another, and now they seemed to be lifelong bosom buddies. Even the hotel staff were nodding in agreement and high-fiving one another.

Tina went on to chronicle a few of her other special moments. In all, she talked nearly an hour at the fundraiser, even though her allocated time was just 20 minutes. Nobody seemed to mind.

After the fundraiser, Tina received many requests for her email address. Some were from people who did not even attend the event but had heard about it from friends or relatives who were there. As I reflected on that afternoon, it was obvious to me that God had used Tina once again to communicate His message.

14

Golden Moments

In September 2006, Tina and I attended the East Texas Fair in Tyler. After sampling some of the famous pies from one of the food stands, Tina excused herself and headed to the restroom. After 20 minutes passed and she had not returned to our designated meeting place, I began to worry that something may have happened to her. I politely asked all the females exiting the restroom if there was still a woman inside the bathroom who was wearing a hat and perhaps needed assistance. One of the ladies I spoke to said there was a woman in the bathroom who was speaking to another lady about cancer. Immediately I knew it was Tina, and she was most likely comforting another cancer patient.

Another 10 minutes went by, and Tina finally came out of the restroom. She was arm in arm with another lady and beaming with excitement. Tina's pale skin was sprinkled with gold dust, and her tone was energetic. She introduced me to her newfound friend, Lisa, who had recently been diagnosed with breast cancer. Lisa was also a patient of Tina's oncologist (imagine that!). The lady apologized for detaining Tina for a short while but said she sincerely appreciated the information Tina provided concerning cancer treatment and the associated mental and physical challenges. It was obvious Tina relished the opportunity to provide encouragement and hope to another cancer patient. The presence of the gold dust on Tina's skin affirmed that God had used Tina for this specific witnessing opportunity. After Tina and I prayed for Lisa, the women exchanged phone numbers and parted ways. I never mentioned the gold dust to Tina.

As we continued our rounds at the fair, Tina picked up a brochure from a local church at one of the exhibit booths. It highlighted that healing services were held at the church the first Sunday of every month. Tina said God was telling her not to miss this opportunity to attend a healing service that was only nine miles from home. We attended the service three days later. It was a full gospel service populated by people of many different backgrounds and cultures. The focus of it was indeed healing as the entire latter half of the service was dedicated to healing prayers and intercession. One by one, all who wanted to come forward and have hands laid on them were welcomed. Without hesitation, Tina and I went forward to receive prayer. After Tina relayed a brief summary of her prayer needs and cancer journey, the lead pastor and support staff laid hands on Tina. As the pastor prayed over her, Tina said she could feel her body temperature rising. Since I was holding Tina's hand during the healing prayer, I was also able to feel the noticeable warmth in her body. As I looked down at her hand, I noticed some gold dust on her skin and also on the pastor's skin. After the pastor finished praying over Tina, we returned to our seats. Tina was noticeably more energetic and had a distinct glow about her. No doubt some divine energy had been transmitted to Tina. Once again, I opted not to inform her of the gold particles that were still glistening on her skin.

Two weeks after the service, Tina underwent the scheduled diagnostic scans to assess her medical condition. The scans revealed that the tumors in her liver and brain were reduced by 50 percent! Other tumors in her body that had been present just a few weeks before were now totally gone! We rejoiced in the good news, and our faith grew even more.

Since our experience at the full gospel church was extremely positive, Tina was anxious to attend more services and events focused on healing. At the request of our three-in-one spiritual partner (friend, neighbor, and prayer intercessor), we decided to attend a revival meeting in Dallas a few days after Thanksgiving. There were four gifted ministers speaking at the event. During the first night of the revival, a woman sitting directly behind Tina placed her hands on Tina's shoulders. She told Tina, "I hope I'm not disturbing you." She kept whispering in Tina's ear that God was telling her to keep her hands on Tina. She said that God told her He loved Tina very much. Tina welcomed the comforting touch and words of endearment. Later, at the hotel, Tina told me that God was going to do something big the next day, so big that no one could deny that it wasn't His work.

The next day we saw the woman from the evening before. Tina asked her, "Have you ever smelled the roses?" Without hesitation the woman said, "No, but I really want to because my name is Sharon Rose." At the hearing of her name, Tina and I looked at each other, and with mouths wide open, we joyfully proclaimed, "The Lord has sent us another messenger to announce we are in the right place." We relayed the significance of the name Rose as it pertains to the Rose of Sharon in the Bible and our experience in the hospital garden the night before Tina's brain surgery. We then told the woman the Lord had given us the name Lily Majestic Ross a few weeks after her brain surgery to indicate His presence at the radiation oncology clinic. Now the Lord had provided another messenger with a unique name that we would readily identify as being from the Lord. That's two names in less than four months to indicate our journey was aligned with our Heavenly Father!

Tina was still reeling from the disclosure of Sharon Rose's name when the evangelist who was speaking at the revival called for all people in attendance with metastatic breast cancer to come forward to the main platform for prayer. Interestingly, he seemed to be looking right at Tina and the section of the multipurpose facility we were sitting in when he made the announcement. Despite Tina's weariness, she jumped up out of her seat in the upper deck of the arena and said, "We are going to the stage." I held Tina's hand as we journeyed downstairs and headed to the main platform. By the time we got there, many people with breast cancer had already gathered at the stage for healing prayer. Tina and I found a spot next to some other folks and waited our turn as the evangelist and some of his support staff made their way across the stage, stopping at each person to pray over them. As the evangelist approached Tina, I turned and looked at her. She had gold sparkles on both of her hands, and her body temperature was rising once again. The evangelist then laid his hands on Tina and lifted her up in prayer.

Tina seemed to have renewed energy after the prayer intercession, and she made the trek back to our seats with much less effort. I didn't make any mention of the gold sparkles on her hands, but Tina apparently saw the gold sparkles on her hands and asked me point-blank, "Did you see the gold dust on my hands and on the hands of the evangelist?" I confirmed the gold dust sighting and relayed that her increased warmth was readily noticeable. As we chatted in our seats, I silently wondered why God was repeatedly using the golden flecks to announce His presence. No doubt, it was easy to see.

Two days later, Tina went back for her blood work and chemo. The lab data indicated that the tumor markers in her blood had dropped 45 points in 28 days. In fact, the tumor markers were now considered to be in the normal range, something that would have been considered impossible just a few months earlier. Upon hearing the positive test results, Tina joyfully proclaimed, "God gives us signs and wonders for others to see His mighty power. These specific signs and wonders, including the provision of gold dust, are for me and my family. God has showered us with His mercy and love and has given us these golden markers to shepherd our journey."

Gold dust sightings seemed to be commonplace in the weeks and months that followed. Many occurred during spiritual events, prayer sessions, and even around the house. The golden sparkles were seen on Tina, our children, prayer warriors, and even me during various activities. One of the more memorable "golden moments" occurred when Tina was telling stories about her good friend Cody who had succumbed to cancer. After Cody's memorial service, Tina was sharing some of her rainbow stories with her friends who had gathered and how Cody's faith had inspired her to keep fighting. Cody had been a walking miracle during the last few years of her life. God had kept her alive with a recipe of divine medicine while the medical community had lost hope. Tina now sensed an opportunity to provide encouragement after the funeral and relayed how God had used Cody to impact the lives around her. As Tina talked, I realized that her recent journey mirrored Cody's. Tina was also fighting an uphill battle, but God was continuing to use her for His glory. God's intervention in Tina's life over the past few years was simply amazing and now had been capped off with some incredible test results that gave us reason to stand up and cheer. As Tina relayed her stories of faith to her friends, including Cody's double rainbow sighting in Colorado, I noticed gold dust on her hands and coat. Yes, another golden moment.

As I pondered the significance of the gold dust on Tina, I silently wondered, *Can others see the gold dust? Was it always there and was I too blind to see it previously? Has my spiritual vision been sharpened so the unseen is now seen?* Whatever the reason, I decided I didn't have to understand the presence of the gold flakes. God placed them on her skin for a reason, and that was good enough for me. If this golden material increased my spiritual acuity and deepened my faith, then this was something I wanted to embrace and talk about. No longer would I be silent about these observations of gold dust and concerned about how people may respond. To the contrary, perhaps this was God's reminder for me to wake up and start seeing things through a spiritual lens.

15

In 2007, Tina's body was being invaded with metastatic breast cancer in various parts of her body. Brain and oral surgeries had addressed high-priority areas to minimize cancer cell migration in the head and mouth. However, it was now time to explore some creative therapies in hopes of providing a systemic solution. Doctors across the country were contacted in hopes of finding another patient like Tina to secure some treatment possibilities.

While doctors combed case histories to find a potential path forward, Tina's body had a chance to recover from the onslaught of chemo and radiation that her body had endured in previous months. Since she had been removed from the clinical trial due to oral cancer, Tina had not received any chemotherapy for nearly three months. As a result, she had renewed physical and mental energy. Despite the lack of an ongoing cancer treatment program during this period, the diagnostic scans and blood work all showed stability. The tumor markers in her blood were down 30 percent, and the brain MRI was significantly better than the previous scan.

The medical community could not explain the unexpected good results. Of course, we attributed the heartwarming news to the handiwork of God. This divine intervention was confirmation for us that God had taken over Tina's healthcare, as well as addressed our worries regarding next steps. It was during this time that a magnet on our refrigerator took on a whole new meaning. It read, "Good Morning! This is God. I will be handling all your problems today. I will not need your help. So, have a good day!" We acknowledged God's sovereignty every time we passed the refrigerator.

During this period, many supernatural events occurred in our lives—many beyond human explanation. It seemed that as we drew closer to God, we received more physical, mental, and spiritual reminders of His presence. One of the most memorable and hard-to-believe things occurred on April 6, 2007. Tina was still in her pajamas and teal-colored robe as she walked in the front yard in the early afternoon. She had her favorite padded slippers on and carried a blue-and-pink fleece blanket around her shoulders for warmth. She had just finished praying on the front porch and had asked the Lord to give her a sign that would convey strength and peace for the unknown journey ahead. When she saw that I was doing yard work in front of our property, she walked toward me and told me about her prayer requests to God.

As we talked about physical stamina and spiritual nourishment on this beautiful April day, a white substance began falling from the sky onto our front yard. Tina exclaimed, "Look! It is manna! God is providing yet again!" As I looked upward, there was a shower of white-gray flakes coming down on my face. The whitish material was neither hot nor cold and not very large. There were no clouds in the sky, so this oddity was not associated with a rain or snow event. I looked around in all directions to see if anybody in our neighborhood was burning anything that would cause white flakes of ash to drift onto our property. However, there was no evidence of fire or smoke anywhere. I then looked out at the cul-de-sac and down the street leading away from our home. To my amazement, the street pavement was completely dry and void of any buildup of a foreign substance. However, our driveway and sidewalk were wet from this material. I raced around the side of the house to see if the whitish substance was falling in the backyard. Lo and behold, it was not "raining" with this material in the backyard either. In the absence of any scientific explanation for this unique atmospheric phenomenon, I nodded in agreement with Tina and proclaimed, "Yep, it's God's handiwork!"

16

The Cross of Life

God's continuing use of signs and wonders was apparent again on March 22, 2008, a day that would forever be etched into my memory. I was working in my home office that sunny afternoon when I heard a loud shout coming from the front door area. It was Tina, and she was screaming with excitement. She barked, "Come outside quickly." I promptly exited the office, scurried down the hall, and made my way out the front door. Upon my arrival outside, Tina boldly pointed to an image in the front yard about 20 feet beyond the front porch and about 10 feet to the left of the sidewalk. The image was of a well-defined cross with a circle around it. Interestingly, our dog was lying between the sidewalk and the cross image that was etched in the yard. He never got up to acknowledge my presence and seemed to have a unique peace about him.

As I studied the position of the cross image from the front porch steps, Tina said she noticed the image when she was sitting on the front-porch swing. She had been reading some Bible passages about how God would make His presence known to His people, and lo and behold, she looked up and saw the image. Tina said she had studied the image intently and noted that it never moved. She also took note that our dog left the front porch where he had been lying and opted to reposition himself near the image. Without a logical explanation, she summoned me after about 20 minutes had elapsed.

As I walked down the front steps and toward the image, our dog remained in place and never moved. The color of the circled cross was a whitish yellow. My initial instinct was that it was simply sunlight reflecting through the trees in the front yard, yielding the unique pattern. This certainly would be a simple explanation to describe the visual oddity. However, upon closer inspection, I noted the color of the cross image was different than the other sunlight images coming through the trees. The cross had a definite whitish tint to it compared to the yellow sunlight patterns that were prevalent elsewhere in the yard. Further, it did not move as the sun changed its position in the southwestern sky. I walked over to the image and touched the grass in the areas highlighted by the cross. The grass temperature was unusually warm and did not reflect the ambient temperature conditions. As a check, I walked over to an area of the yard where sunlight was prevalent on the ground, and the temperature was noticeably cooler. The temperature difference was indeed puzzling. It seemed that the elevated temperature of the cross image might actually burn a cross pattern into the grass.

I decided to sit and watch the cross image for an extended period of time to ensure that it was not simply a collection of shadows highlighting the cross pattern. This test would at least satisfy my intellectual curiosity and utilize my engineering background. After nearly an hour (not counting the 20 minutes after Tina's initial observation) the image had *not* moved while the other sunlight-shadow patterns moved in accordance with the declining afternoon sun. I decided this was a unique event with no logical explanation other than it was divinely inspired. It seemed God had provided yet another sign of His glorious presence in our lives. To document this unique sighting, we took several pictures of the cross. I made sure I got a few photos that showed our dog resting peacefully next to the cross.

After taking the pictures, I returned to the house to resume my work activities. According to Tina, the cross disappeared after she went indoors. Not surprisingly, the cross was the main topic of conversation at the dinner table that night. Our youngest son was still intrigued about the visual display. The cross also seemed to give Tina a new source of energy. We took the pictures of the cross image to church the following day. We showed them to everyone in our Bible class, as well as to several members of the church. All the people who saw the pictures were genuinely intrigued. Some interesting conversations ensued afterward.

A few weeks later, the leader of our men's Bible class called and asked if he could take a copy of the cross picture on his mission trip to Bosnia. I gladly said yes and gave him a copy. After he returned from the mission trip a few weeks later, he called and informed me that he got more mileage out of that picture than anything else he said or did. Although I was pleased to know that the photo played an important role on the mission trip, I wondered why people of different backgrounds and beliefs would respond so favorably to the picture. Perhaps it was nothing more complicated than for people's basic desire to see a picture of God's handiwork.

In the months that followed, I received many requests for a copy of the picture. Whether the picture requests were driven by a thirst for heavenly signs and wonders or simply a response to an intellectual curiosity, I will never know. However, the picture seemed to provide encouragement and hope for many people. If that was God's intention for His visual display, then it was good enough for me.

17

A New State of Mind

The year 2008 would be a remarkable year in Tina's life. As it turned out, it would also be her last year on earth. Nonetheless, God continued to use her in mighty ways. Despite her own health challenges, she never stopped reaching out and ministering to those around her. Waiting rooms in doctors' offices frequently became havens for spreading the gospel. It seemed someone sitting by Tina would always inquire what she was reading and why she had a smile on her face. During these moments, I simply smiled at Tina and nodded that it was time for her witness. Tina would always respond by saying she was reading the best book, and then she would show them the Bible. Time in the waiting room always seemed to pass quickly while she encouraged fellow patients. Her infectious personality and zeal for the Lord made her a magnet for attracting people who needed to know there was still life yet to be lived. By the time Tina was called back to the doctor's office for her appointment, she had likely shared the gospel with many people.

There were many instances where clinic staff asked Tina to talk to patients undergoing chemo before or after her appointment. She gladly accepted the invitations, even if the news she received about her own condition was less than favorable. I distinctly remember one occasion when an older man asked Tina what it was like to undergo chemotherapy. He was obviously having difficulty accepting his current health situation, and his downtrodden face spoke volumes. Without revealing the extent of her cancer journey (now 13 years and counting), she politely said, "I have experienced a few of those." She then provided some words of encouragement and quoted some Bible passages. We then prayed over the man and asked God to provide peace in his life.

As much as God provided spiritual energy to Tina during this time, he seemed to equip Tina's prayer warriors even more. Most of her prayer intercessors were still members of the women's prayer group she had been part of several years earlier. These ladies were simply amazing, and they were always willing to drop what they were doing if I relayed that it was time to lift Tina up. I gladly joined their prayer circle when they arrived at the house. To this day, I have learned more about prayer and the spiritual world from these women than any other group I have been around. Perhaps that was God's way of ministering to me.

During our quiet times at the house during Tina's farewell year, I often sat in our living room and listened to Tina play her piano. She had been an accomplished pianist since childhood, and I had the opportunity to buy her a Yamaha grand piano for Christmas in 2005. I will never forget the look on her face as the delivery truck made its way up our driveway that day. She was so excited when she realized what was being delivered. Now that same piano in 2008 was providing a calmness that seemed to combat whatever uneasiness she may have been feeling. Her favorite song she liked to play was Billy Joel's "New York State of Mind." I was never sure if it was the lyrics, the musical composition, or the artist that attracted her to that song. In any case, she always played it with such passion. It seemed the song was now facilitating a "new state of mind" in her that was centered squarely on Christ. After Tina's death, I passed the cherished piano on to Andrew. The picture shows Tina and Andrew playing a song together.

18

New Beginnings

Tina's health declined as 2008 progressed, but I never seemed to be worried. I had seen so many miracles in her life, and it was obvious that God was using her for a greater purpose. Perhaps my lack of health insecurities regarding Tina was also due to the divine peace God had previously given me. Whatever the reason, 13 years of watching a woman successfully navigate through the ups and downs of cancer while relying on God for guidance and direction had aligned me with His purpose for her life. As such, I never dwelled on potential loss-of-life scenarios. In addition, Tina always seemed to be able to keep pace with many of her normal activities. Her Wonder Woman endurance always seemed to propel her forward, and the sight of a rainbow or other divine wonder simply provided a recharge of her batteries. Her presence at the finish line of the Komen Tyler Race for the Cure in May gave us additional assurance that she was, indeed, a survivor.

During the summer of 2008, however, she began to slow down mentally and physically. Speaking sessions were eventually

confined to the front porch and inside the house. Her lack of appetite and thirst began to catch up with her. That led to a reduced energy level and a few trips to the hospital due to dehydration. Her declining health was difficult to see on a day-to-day basis. However, I am sure it was easier for other folks to see who checked in at less frequent intervals.

My first in-your-face moment regarding Tina's declining physical state was during a brief conversation with my spiritual mentor and Bible class teacher. He was a retired physician and had lost his first wife to pancreatic cancer, so he was used to seeing the typical end-of-life signs. After church one day, he asked if I had picked out a cemetery plot for Tina. After pausing for a moment, I said no. His body language and tone suggested it was time to start making those preparations. He didn't need to say anything else.

As God gradually opened my eyes to see Tina's frailty, I began to focus on her upcoming birthday on August 8. This year it would be celebrated as 8/8/08. This unique date stamp gave me reason to believe that something special was going to happen that day. Would God provide yet another healing miracle? Would another rainbow appear? Would another revival of the soul occur?

Tina's family, friends, and I began planning a surprise birthday party for her. We decided to have it at a local café and bakery. I knew the owner, and she was more than willing to let us host the party at her place of business, even though she was normally closed on Saturday afternoons. The owner and her family were true believers, and Tina and I frequently had the chance to pray with them. Their business also had delivered food to the hospital for our family and out-of-town guests when Tina had her brain surgery. We dearly loved these folks, and we were anxious to decorate the party room in the café when the time came. The only issue was keeping the party a secret. I had never planned a surprise birthday party for Tina in 23 years of marriage, and I did not want this opportunity to slip away.

Tina's parents drove from Missouri to provide support and help celebrate her pending birthday party. We agreed to take Tina to a late lunch at a restaurant on the big day while others gathered at the café and provided last-minute decorations. When we finished eating, we drove to the café under the premise of picking up some goodies and saying hello to the owner. Fortunately, Tina had no idea that a surprise party was at hand when she opened the door to the party room. She was overcome with joy as she scanned the room filled with more than 30 friends, family, prayer warriors, church members, and healthcare workers.

Although I had an expectation that a few folks might want to say some words about Tina before the typical birthday party activities commenced, I had no inkling that God was about to use this event as a spiritual revival of sorts. One by one, everyone in attendance gave a brief testimony of how Tina had impacted their life and brought them closer to God. Many of them had prepared written remarks to convey their feelings and love for Tina. They easily could have spoken for 20 minutes or more but gladly yielded to others in the interest of time. There was not a dry eye in the café as people gave their testimonies and prayed. Perhaps the biggest moment of the afternoon came when our youngest

son, Grant, who was 16 at the time and not one to publicly voice his feelings, opened up and shared his heart for his mom. That certainly brought tears to everyone. By the time everyone had a chance to speak and honor Tina and her faith in God and Jesus Christ, nearly two hours had passed.

We finally got around to cutting the cake and opening birthday gifts. The cake was decorated with the words "Happy Birthday Tina, 8-8-08, New Beginnings." The decoration was a reference to a painting Tina had done in 2006 titled *Beauty from Ashes (New Beginnings)* that featured eight red tulips arising from a black bed. Tina smiled when she saw the cake inscription and remarked, "Yes, this is a new beginning. I don't know what God has in store for me, but I can't wait to see."

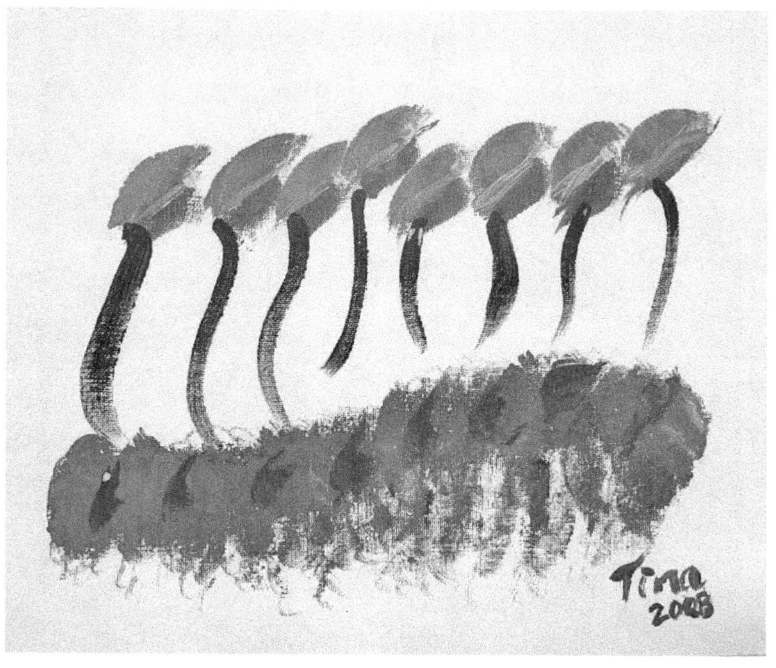

19

Nearing the Finish Line

Although Tina's health continued to deteriorate during the summer and fall of 2008, I was still somewhat oblivious that the end of her life was near. After all, I had witnessed miracle after miracle for nearly 14 years, and who was I to say the incredible run would not continue for many more? God continued to use Tina in many ways to spread the gospel to those around her. It wasn't until one evening while I was working at the office that I sensed real urgency in her situation. She called to tell me it was time to come home. Tina rarely called me at work, so the fact that she called was a red flag. Her voice was noticeably frail during our brief conversation and trailed off before I could say, "I'm on my way." Upon my arrival at the house, I found Tina extremely dehydrated. She had barely consumed any liquids while I was away, and her softened eyes told a story that maybe the battle was nearing the end.

The next day, I called the doctor's office and said that Tina was not drinking any liquids. Her oncologist told me to bring her to the clinic as soon as possible. As I gathered up essentials for the visit, I noticed Tina was very pale and weak. I held her hand tightly as we exited the house and walked through the garage to my Chevrolet Suburban that was parked in the driveway. As we made our way through the garage, I noticed our beloved dog, Blu, sitting at attention as Tina passed by. The significance of that did not elude me as I had always heard that animals were able to sense when humans were hurting. It seemed that Blu knew this was probably the last time he was going to see his favorite female companion. His military-like posture as he sat motionless was clearly meant to convey respect and thanks.

I managed to get Tina into the truck and then transported her to the oncology clinic. She was subsequently placed in the hospital after receiving several units of intravenous fluids. One of the attendants said she was lucky to be alive since she was severely dehydrated. Although I expected Tina to return home within a few days after her body chemistry stabilized, it seemed the progression of cancer had accelerated, causing her to need additional testing.

I called Tina's parents and told them they needed to come to Texas to support their daughter. Although I didn't convey any emotional distress, I suspected they knew the end was near. They wasted little time leaving their home in Missouri and driving to Texas. I was glad when they arrived since the responsibilities of managing home life, work, and caretaking were starting to be overwhelming.

As the hospital continued to run a battery of tests, I began to realize that Tina may not come home. Her weakened state was apparent, and her normal infectious enthusiasm was operating at a significantly reduced level. Prayer warriors began to show up at key intervals and frequently contacted me for status updates to ensure proper coverage. I remember going to the hospital chapel one afternoon and praying with Suzanne, Tina's spiritual momma. We had prayed together many times before, but this time it seemed the atmosphere was different. We walked to the front of the chapel and dropped to our knees. Sensing I probably was going to have difficulty verbalizing my prayers, she quickly commenced intercessory prayer, and we held hands as she prayed. As she proclaimed the sovereign power of Jesus in our lives and His mighty role in Tina's healthcare journey, I began to feel a warming sensation enter my body through our joined hands. As she continued to speak with such conviction, it seemed my body temperature kept rising. By the time she requested the healing power of God to protect Tina's body, my forehead was literally dripping with sweat. When she finished her prayer, it seemed all I could do was give her a hug and say, "Yes, it's all about the blood."

As we got up from our knees, it seemed all the energy had been drained from me. As we turned to walk down the aisle toward the back of the chapel, I noticed the reflection of a rainbow on one of the pews near the front of the church where we had been praying. It was obviously a result of light being refracted through one of the stained-glass windows. I pointed to the colorful pattern on the surface of the pew and told my prayer partner, "I believe your prayer was heard." She nodded in agreement as she was aware of the significance of rainbows on Tina's journey.

The next day, the hospital staff advised me that they wanted to run another X-ray on her chest region to confirm her current condition. At this point, I was unsure if Tina was even strong enough to endure another test. Repeated blood work, CT scans, and other diagnostic tests over the past several days had sapped whatever energy she seemed to have left. It was now apparent that the hospital and doctors were looking to me for Tina's healthcare decisions. This moment marked the first time in Tina's cancer journey that I was solely responsible for her treatment. I felt all alone at that moment, and I walked up to Tina's father in the hallway near her hospital room to seek his guidance. He obviously sensed my dilemma regarding the need for any additional testing. Although he said to do whatever was best for Tina, his body language suggested that enough testing had already been done, and it was now in God's hands. We prayed together for a few minutes to gain some clarity. No doubt, I needed some input from God on this. As I contemplated this all-important decision, I kept thinking back to the many private moments Tina and I had had. We agreed to keep fighting as long as God was still using her to proclaim His glory. As I reflected on that commitment, I concluded that the additional X-ray was needed to confirm the path forward. Tina had never given up, so I was not about to start by declining a test that may prove useful. I felt peace about this decision, and I gave the okay to proceed.

20

She's Home!

Tina remained on the oncology floor of the hospital for the remainder of the evening but was transferred to the intensive care unit (ICU) during the early morning hours the next day. It was now Wednesday, November 5, 2008.

I arrived at the hospital early in the morning as I usually did to talk with the doctors during their morning rounds. There were now multiple doctors involved with Tina's care. Besides her beloved oncologist, a critical care doctor and ICU staff were now involved. Other specialists were also working behind the scenes. As I entered Tina's ICU room, which was separate from the other critical care rooms, I noted she was hooked up to an array of diagnostic equipment that recorded her vitals and other information. She was alert and easily recognized me but was obviously having difficulty breathing. The ICU radiology team came in while I was there and performed another chest X-ray with a mobile imaging machine. It was obvious to me now that the doctors were worried about fluid buildup in her lungs. Tina had her lungs drained twice in recent years, so I was fully aware of the impact of metastatic breast cancer on fluid buildup in the lungs and the surrounding pulmonary cavity. The first time her lungs were drained, they removed nearly two quarts of fluid from her body. She breathed a lot easier after that procedure. It now appeared that fluid buildup was occurring again. I also noticed her feet and legs were beginning to swell.

Tina's parents were already at the hospital when I arrived, and we discussed Tina's current status. We agreed that they would stay with Tina during the morning, provide emotional support, and tend to any requests she may have. I agreed to pick up Tina's aunt from the airport in Dallas later that morning. Tina's parents had summoned her a few days earlier, and she was now flying to Texas in hopes of seeing Tina one last time. After I kissed Tina and said a quick prayer, I told her I would be back with Aunt Mary Lou by early afternoon. I then left the hospital to begin my journey to Dallas.

About halfway to Dallas, I received a call on my cell phone from Tina's oncologist. She said if Tina did not improve, she would not be able to remove her from the ICU and get her back on the oncology floor of the hospital. She then proceeded to tell me the prospects were not good for her survival. I distinctly remember where I was on Interstate 20 the moment Tina's oncologist forewarned of Tina's pending death. I was in the right-hand lane of Interstate 20 between Canton and Terrell heading west. I was driving the speed limit of 70 mph, and traffic was fairly heavy. I immediately started to tear up as traffic whizzed by me on the left. It took all I had to keep it together and operate my Suburban safely in traffic. I was tempted to pull over and collect my thoughts, but then I remembered that I still had to pick up Tina's aunt at the airport. So I continued onward toward Dallas. To this day, I cannot pass that location on Interstate 20 without thinking of that moment when the doctor called me.

I managed to make it safely to Dallas Love Field. My timing was nearly perfect since Aunt Mary Lou was just emerging from the doors to the baggage claim area. We made eye contact, and I pulled over in the parking area designated for passenger arrivals. I loaded her bags in the back of the Suburban, and we quickly exited the congested loading area. Aside from the initial greetings at the airport, we did not speak a word to each other. I could sense Tina's aunt knew I was hurting and didn't know quite how to break the ice. Finally, after 10 minutes passed, she got up the courage to ask, "How is Tina doing?" I simply responded, "She is dying." That was the first time I ever used the word *dying* regarding Tina's cancer journey. After my dire response, we engaged in limited conversation. Tina's aunt did most of the talking as I focused on driving and thoughts of Tina. As Mary Lou talked, I realized what her purpose for the trip was. Although her primary motivation for coming to Texas was to visit Tina, it now seemed her main purpose was to minister to me. Her natural mothering skills provided a calmness that I sorely needed. I am sure God orchestrated that, and I silently thanked her for the comforting words and companionship.

About 20 minutes from Tyler, I received a frantic phone call from my mother-in-law. She was obviously in an emotional state and said the doctors and hospital personnel were asking questions that were uncomfortable for her. I advised her that I would be there shortly to answer any questions. After we arrived at the hospital, we quickly made our way to the ICU wing. I was greeted by medical staff who wanted to know if I was responsible for Tina's healthcare decisions. I responded in the affirmative and quickly went to Tina's ICU room. By now, Tina's entire body had swelled up. Her puffy cheeks and face told a different story than just five hours earlier when I had left the hospital. I scanned her vital signs and noted that a ventilator was now controlling her breathing. The ICU doctor on shift came into the room and gave me an update on Tina's condition. He inquired if I had a medical directive for Tina, and I said yes. I responded that God, not a machine, would decide if Tina was to continue her journey on earth. He then indicated that it would be a good time to gather close friends and relatives as the end was drawing near.

As I recoiled from the doctor's medical update and guidance, I advised Tina's parents that I would alert my two sons, sister-in-law, and a few prayer warriors to come to the hospital within the next few hours. My sister-in-law, Kim, lived the farthest away, so I was insistent that our final gathering with Tina would not occur before she arrived. One by one, I called each of the people on my must-call list and told them to drop what they were doing and get to the hospital as soon as they could. Andrew said his girlfriend wanted to come, too, since Tina had been an important influence in her life. Grant was in high school, and his school gladly released him to come to the hospital. The hardest phone call was to Tina's sister, Kim. She was driving from Houston to Lafayette, Louisiana, that day to visit her best friend, but I advised her to head north and not east since it was time to say goodbye to her beloved sister.

After I made all the necessary phone calls, I left the ICU area and walked to an outside garden on the hospital grounds near the chapel. After saying a short prayer, I sat down on a concrete bench in the garden and called my mother in Missouri. When she answered the phone, I was unable to verbalize any greeting. Before I could produce any words, my mother said, "What's wrong, Bill?" (Isn't it amazing how mothers know what's on their child's heart without even seeing or hearing them?) I simply responded, "Tina's dying." I started to cry, and I know she was crying, too, due to the prolonged silence on the phone. "Do you want me to come?" she asked. I said, "No, she will already be with the Lord by the time you get here."

After talking with my mom and a few friends who had called to check on Tina, I made my way back to the ICU. By now, Andrew and his girlfriend had arrived. Grant was also there, as well as most of the people I had contacted. At my request, Andrew brought a guitar with him so he could play a few songs for his mother. Andrew seemed comfortable playing in this setting, so I didn't feel any uneasiness about invoking his musical gifts. He sang a couple of family-favorite tunes at his mother's bedside as the afternoon gave way to evening. I will never forget the smile on Tina's face as she listened to her son playing softly. Although the backdrop for this scene was certainly not one you would want to intentionally create for poetic purposes, the atmosphere was nonetheless precious. Perhaps it was at this point that the passion Tina spoke with for many years was transferred to Andrew and lived out in his future career as a praise and worship leader.

After all the designated family and friends arrived, we gathered around Tina's bed in her ICU room. The curtains were drawn, and the ICU staff closed the door to ensure our privacy. I advised the family that we would sing a few songs to honor the Lord, and then each of them would have an opportunity to share whatever was on their hearts regarding Tina.

As I looked around the room, the significance of the moment was not lost on me. A peace came over me as I looked at all the familiar faces. We then proceeded to sing "Amazing Grace" and "How Great Thou Art." The lyrics seemed more powerful than normal as we sang the timeless hymns. The beautiful harmonies filled the room, and it seemed that Tina was smiling nearly the entire time. At the completion of the last song, we joined hands and then commenced to honor Tina through prayer and testimonies. I don't recall what each person said in their goodbye words, but the heartfelt response of each person was simply beautiful. Although the words voiced by each were different, everyone acknowledged the depth of Tina's love for the Lord. When it was my turn to provide the final blessing, I said something akin to "Lord, it is time for Tina to lay down her cross and put it at Your feet. She has boldly testified to Your glory. All we ask is that You pick up her cross and bring her home to You." Within two minutes, God called her home as evidenced by the heart monitors and other medical equipment in the room. Tina had indeed left her home on earth and crossed that heavenly bridge to her eternal home with Jesus. *Thank you, Lord, for hearing our prayers and bringing her home in a timely manner for us to see!* The time was 9:40 p.m.

As the family stood around the bed and reflected on Tina's passing, there understandably were tears. However, the tears were not simply of sadness but also of joy. God had clearly orchestrated her final moments on earth, and we got to be a witness to that. It gave me such peace knowing she was now with Jesus and was seeing Him face-to-face.

As it turned out, there were a lot more witnesses to her passing than just those of us gathered in Tina's ICU room. Little did we know that the ICU staff, other hospital personnel, friends, fellow church members, and some visitors had gathered in the ICU wing when they heard the singing. Apparently, some of them even joined in to sing the familiar choral refrains. No doubt, God had used this setting to minister to people we did not even know. As I walked out of Tina's room, one of the ICU staff came up to me and said that was a beautiful way to honor my wife and create a loving picture from a difficult situation. I simply replied that it was God's handiwork, not mine.

The reality of Tina's passing was quickly brought to the forefront as hospital staff asked where I wanted her body to be taken. Of course, I had never pondered this detail previously. I had firmly believed just 24 hours earlier that Tina would still be here with us and not in heaven. After contemplating this question for a moment, I advised them to take the body to a funeral home near my house. It was new and seemed to be the most convenient location for the family.

After completing all the necessary paperwork, I finally made my way out of ICU. Everyone else had already left the hospital, so it was just me who remained to collect my personal items and drive home. Due to the late hour, it was dark outside as I made my way to my vehicle. It was at that moment that I realized I would be driving home for the first time without my companion of 24 years.

As I began to sense my current state of exhaustion, I paused for a moment to seek the Lord's counsel one more time on this long emotional day. I prayed that the Lord would give me strength to make it home safely and keep me focused on Him now and forever. I also asked God to give me a sign that Tina was no longer in pain and was in heaven seeing Jesus face-to-face. As I finished the prayer and exited the hospital parking lot, I turned on the radio. The song "There Will Be a Day" by Jeremy Camp was playing. I simply smiled to myself. I was very familiar with the lyrics of that song, especially the chorus. Those words were exactly what I needed to hear. *Thank you, Lord!*

21

A Guiding Light

I woke up the next morning around 10:00. The funeral home called, and they were eager to start the funeral arrangements. I told them I would gather a few folks and stop by their facility later that afternoon. I had decided to take my father-in-law and sister-in-law with me for their input on any decisions.

As I ate breakfast with the various members of the family who had stayed overnight at the house, I decided it was a good idea to break the tension and ask each one what their fondest memory of Tina was. Each person had a different memory of Tina, and it was good to hear the stories that went along with their recollections. Although everyone seemed a little tired, the general pulse of the family was good. Whether this was because Tina's passing had been anticipated or whether we all accepted God's provision for Tina to be called home, it really didn't matter. The glue that had held this family together for many years and would continue to hold it together was our faith in God. We ended our morning conversation with prayer.

My father-in-law, sister-in-law, and I made our way to the funeral home. After answering numerous questions and filling out information sheets, we went downstairs to the area where the caskets were displayed. I solicited the input of my two companions regarding their casket preference. They didn't seem to have any strong opinions. However, I immediately locked in on a beautiful white casket. Although it was relatively expensive, it simply reminded me of Tina and her beauty and the purity of Christ. Both nodded in agreement as I told the attendant we would take the pearl-white casket.

We then made our way to the cemetery I had decided to use for burial purposes. It was located at the south end of Tyler and was the closest cemetery to our house. I checked in at the cemetery office and advised the attendant that we were seeking a burial plot for my wife. I didn't have any preference at this point for a desired plot location, but to jump-start our search, I asked the lady if she could show me the location of the Hurst burial plots. Dr. Hurst was my spiritual mentor and friend. He was the one who had asked me if I had made burial plans for Tina two months before she died. In response to my query, the office attendant handed me a map of the cemetery and indicated that the Hurst graves were in the back part of the cemetery on the left-hand side near the woods.

We drove to the area highlighted by the cemetery representative and parked in the cul-de-sac. We then started walking to the area where the Hurst plots were believed to be. After several minutes, my father-in-law found the headstone of Dr. and Mrs. Hurst. It was located along the south side of a sidewalk in the back of the cemetery. Across the sidewalk on the north side were several available spaces that could be selected as possible gravesites. As I pondered this area and looked around at other potential gravesites in the immediate vicinity, it suddenly occurred to me that I needed to select the two spaces directly across the sidewalk from the Hursts. This location made complete sense since Mrs. Hurst had been a spiritual mentor to Tina before her passing, and Dr. Hurst had certainly been a spiritual mentor to me. At that moment, I visualized Tina's final resting place across from Mrs. Hurst and my (future) resting place across from Dr. Hurst.

I advised my father-in-law and sister-in-law that I felt drawn to this specific area, but I needed confirmation from the Lord. As such, the three of us joined hands and stood in the designated area across the sidewalk from the Hursts' graves. I asked the Lord to give us a sign that the plots we were standing on were indeed the desired burial sites for Tina and me. As we were praying for confirmation of the burial location on this partly cloudy day, the sun suddenly emerged from behind the clouds and began to shine brightly through the pine trees that surrounded the cemetery in this area. There was a definite column of sunlight highlighting the ground we were standing on. The instant warmth on my head and back from the sun was like a laser beam into my soul. No doubt, this was a clear sign that God was giving a thumbs-up on the burial location. I looked at my father-in-law and sister-in-law and asked if they felt incredible warmth in their bodies. They acknowledged the divinely inspired warmth, and tears came to my eyes. I concluded the prayer by giving thanks to the Lord for the timely confirmation. I then looked up into the sky and noticed the sun had now retreated behind the clouds once again.

As we walked away from the chosen gravesites, I realized that God was still looking after us and directing our path after Tina's death. A decision that could have been extremely difficult and potentially taken months to finalize had just been completed in a few minutes. All we had to do was ask the Lord for help. For those who say God never works in an expeditious manner, I beg to differ.

22

Although the day after Tina's death had already been filled with several activities orchestrated by God, His handiwork was further made evident as we arrived home from the cemetery. Upon entering the house, I made my way to the office to get some alone time and catch up on emails and texts. As I scrolled through the messages, I noticed I had received a text from Tina's oncologist early in the morning while I was sleeping. She was apparently making her rounds in the hospital when she noticed a double rainbow in the glass of one of the corridor windows. She stopped and took a picture of the image and then sent it to me.

When I called to thank her for the picture, she mentioned she had been thinking of Tina at that moment in the corridor and the impact Tina had had on her. She then looked up and saw the double rainbow in the window. She said she screamed with excitement as she took the picture and knew I would want a copy of the rainbow image. I acknowledged the rainbow and said that was definitely a godsend. Perhaps it was also Tina's way of sending her love from heaven. However, what was more interesting in the picture was the small image of Tina in the background next to the doctor's face. I remarked, "I love the image of Tina in the background. How cool is that!" The doctor replied, "What image?" I advised her to look at the picture again. I told her it was easy to see the doctor's image reflected in the window, but there was also a small image of Tina in the background. She replied, "Wow! I missed that!" We agreed that the unique image of Tina could not be explained by any ordinary means. To this day, I cannot explain how Tina's image made its way into the picture taken by the doctor. Once again, I will chalk it up to divine intervention. Clearly it was meant to provide hope and encouragement.

As I showed the picture to the rest of the family, they were equally enthusiastic. No one had seen such a unique picture before, nor could they explain the appearance of Tina in the picture. It was the topic of conversation for a few hours.

As I silently thanked the Lord for another sign from above, I received a phone call from a friend of ours who had heard of Tina's passing. He called to extend his condolences and check on me and the family. He said he was in Latin America doing some mission work. He then proceeded to tell me a highly unusual event that had occurred the evening before. He said he and a few others had been making the rounds in a hospital in Nicaragua and were praying over people with various illnesses. During a prayer session in one of the hospital rooms, he said he saw a vision of a woman in the room who looked strikingly similar to Tina. He said the angelic being was clothed in white and was wearing a hat much like the one Tina used to wear. He indicated he felt such peace with the "visitor" as if he already knew her. He said the heavenly creature was focused on the man in the hospital bed and appeared to be an intense prayer warrior. After my friend finished his story about the strange encounter, I asked him, "What time did this occur?" In response he said, "I do remember the time because I looked at my watch when I first noticed the vision. It was 9:40 p.m." My mouth dropped open. That was the exact time of Tina's passing. I paused for a moment and then said, "Do you want to guess what time Tina died?" The response came quickly from my friend. "9:40 p.m." I said, "Yep."

As I hung up the phone, I tried to process the meaning of what I had just heard. A multitude of questions entered my mind. *Lord, what is the meaning of all these signs and wonders? Was the image that my friend saw in Nicaragua really Tina? Could it really be that Tina was in a hospital bed in Tyler, Texas, experienced physical death, crossed over into heaven, and then was providing heavenly prayer support in a Latin American hospital all in the same day? Lord, I need help with this, but I will leave it to You as part of Your plan.* My thoughts then gravitated to this familiar Bible passage: "Trust in the LORD with all your heart and lean not on your own understanding; in all your ways submit to him, and he will make your paths straight" (Prov. 3:5–6).

As I reflected on the events that had transpired that day, the only explanation that seemed to make any sense was that the signs and wonders were divinely inspired and that God is firmly in control. I may never understand the heavenly visions from a human perspective, and that is all right. I just need to seek Him so He will direct my path.

23

A Multigenerational Celebration Service

Tina went to her eternal home on a Wednesday. However, the memorial service would not be held until the following Monday so our former pastor from Houston could attend and preside over the service. The good news was that it enabled us to have four full days to plan a celebration service.

There was never any discussion over what type of service the event would be. It was a foregone conclusion that the service would *not* be a somber funeral with the typical elements. On the contrary, it would be a high-energy service that would celebrate Tina's life on earth and, more importantly, highlight her heavenly homecoming.

I asked Andrew if he felt comfortable putting the music program together for the service. Although I knew he was fully capable of accomplishing this task due to his musical gifting, I was mentally prepared that he may have some reservations about performing at a memorial service for his mother. However, he readily accepted the invitation, and I simply deferred to him for all music-related items. My only contribution in the music area was relaying a few songs I knew Tina would want to be played.

With Andrew handling the music portion, that left me to focus on the rest of the memorial service. The to-do list included lining up speakers, preparing a video presentation of Tina's life, getting programs made, preparing an outline of the service, finalizing Scripture readings, and coordinating with the pastors and our church.

I focused on the speakers first. After praying for guidance in this area, God revealed to me that a multigenerational lineup should be used to cover the speaking roles. That certainly made sense because Tina had witnessed to young and old alike. Not including folks from different age groups might preclude some important testimonies and perspectives. After contemplating potential speaking candidates, I decided to use a young girl, a middle-aged woman, and an older man. The young girl was the daughter of a lady who cleaned our house for several years. Tina frequently talked with the girl when she came to the house with her mother on cleaning days. She was well spoken for her age and had a heart for the Lord. The middle-aged woman worked at the Tyler Cancer Center and got to know Tina well. She had many opportunities to interact with Tina at the chemotherapy clinic and got to know her on a personal and spiritual level. The older man simply was a godsend. When I called to ask him to speak, he said it would be an honor since Tina had ministered to him and his wife during a very difficult time in their lives. Although I had a backup list prepared in case one or more of the selected people were not available, it seemed God took care of that. All three speakers were pleased to participate and welcomed the opportunity.

I contacted our church to inquire about hosting the celebration service in the worship center. Church representatives were very accommodating and told us that Tina's service would be the first memorial service held at the church. That was not surprising since the church was relatively new and comprised of primarily younger families. I must admit, however, it was an odd feeling knowing that Tina's service would be the first memorial service there. As such, there were no church protocols or precedents that had been established for memorial services.

After finalizing the date, time, and location of the celebration service, I began drafting a program for the service. The photo for the front cover was a no-brainer. The perfect picture was the photo Tina's oncologist relayed to me the morning after her death. It contained the elements that showcased her cancer journey—a double rainbow, her oncologist, mountains, and an image of Tina in the background to highlight her beauty. The picture also seemed to impart hope and convey the message that anything is possible with the help of God. Obviously, I had to include Jeremiah 29:11–13 as one of the Scripture readings. Those verses were central to Tina's life and had been given to her by God through prayer intercessors. For the last song of the service, I had to go with the powerful worship song "Mighty to Save" by Hillsong. We loved that song and still do!

I then contacted the pastor from our old church in Nassau Bay to confirm his availability. We agreed to meet the night before the memorial service at a hotel in Tyler to share a few memories and discuss service details. During our visit in the hotel lobby, I asked him what his most vivid memories of Tina were. He responded with two stories. The first one was associated with a church board meeting when Tina was the treasurer of the Board of Directors. The focus of the meeting was to review and approve the proposed church budget for the following year. The budget review led to a discussion on tithing and the need for church members to examine their personal situations and align their contributions with the tithing benchmark. After hearing resistance from some board members regarding the need to tithe, Tina challenged all the board members to follow the biblical example of tithing and walk by faith. According to the pastor, her comments were uncomfortable for some but were readily endorsed by others. He indicated that Tina's comments were necessary to reset the tone of the meeting and properly frame the issue of giving and tithing.

The second story involved Tina's testimony at the church in the late 1990s. He recalled giving a sermon based on the text in Romans 5:1–5.

> *Therefore, since we have been justified through faith, we have peace with God through our Lord Jesus Christ, through whom we have gained access by faith into this grace in which we now stand. And we boast in the hope of the glory of God. Not only so, but we also glory in our sufferings, because we know that suffering produces perseverance; perseverance, character; and character, hope. And hope does not put us to shame, because God's love has been poured out into our hearts through the Holy Spirit, who has been given to us.*

The pastor indicated that the topics of suffering, perseverance, character, and hope provided a natural segue to Tina's testimony since she had experienced or demonstrated all these things on her journey. He remembered Tina speaking with such passion as she proclaimed the healing power of the blood of Jesus Christ.

The impact of Tina on others did not fully hit home until I saw the turnout at her visitation the day before the celebration service. There were people standing in line at the funeral home before the visitation even officially began. I distinctly remember the gentleman who was first in line. I had worked with him nearly a decade earlier. He was a kind and gentle soul, and I had gotten to know him well at the office and on business trips. He had driven four hours from Houston to attend the visitation and pay his respects. I was deeply moved by his attendance since he had only met Tina a few times. Nonetheless, his limited interactions with her were memorable and obviously had an impact on him.

I don't know how I managed to stand on my feet for more than three hours at the visitation and greet all the guests. I guess God managed all of that. I just remember looking over at Tina in the casket several times and thinking, *We still make a great team.* My silent comment was a reference to the number of times Tina and I had attended conferences, fundraisers, political events, and other social gatherings, and used a team approach to meet people and accomplish objectives. The team was obviously split up now, but we were still meeting people, albeit under unwanted circumstances.

At last, the day came for the celebration service. It was an overcast day. The service was scheduled to start at 10:00 a.m. at the church. The company I worked for and helped start in 2004 had given permission for all employees to attend the service. This was a nice gesture and reflected the family culture the company was founded on. I was honored that most of the employees attended the service.

The worship center was arranged in its normal configuration. The familiar layout was comprised of three sections with an aisle between each section. The first couple of rows in each area were reserved for family members. Somehow, I got positioned on the front row on the far right all by myself. That was because both of my sons were onstage as part of the music team. Members of my wife's family, my siblings, my mother, and other relatives that made the trip to Tyler were seated in the rows behind me. I must admit I felt a little alone under the circumstances due to the seating arrangements.

The service started with a welcome by one of the pastors of our church. His remarks were followed by several worship songs. It was customary in our family to stand during the worship portion of a church service. Singing songs of praise and standing just went hand in hand. Accordingly, I was standing while Andrew and the music team played the worship songs. The music team included Grant, Andrew's girlfriend, and some other family friends and musicians. After 10 or 15 minutes into the music portion of the service, I was told that everybody in attendance was still standing out of respect for me. It seemed I was in worship mode and was oblivious to the need for some people to sit. One of the ushers came up to me and said I might want to sit down so the folks in attendance who had physical limitations could resort to sitting while at the same time being respectful to me. In response to the request, I gladly sat down and continued to sing the songs Andrew had prepared.

The songs of celebration were followed by a picture presentation that highlighted Tina's life. If truth be told, I probably had way too many pictures in the presentation that lasted nearly 20 minutes. Nonetheless, I think nearly all the folks in attendance enjoyed seeing pictures of Tina at various stages of her life—as a child, a pianist, a young adult, a homecoming queen, a beauty pageant contestant, a wife, a mother, a cancer survivor, an orator, a prayer warrior, and a loving follower of Jesus Christ.

After Tina's obituary was read, the testimonies were next on the agenda. I am not sure what my expectations were for this part of the service. However, I knew it was going to be impactful and that God would use these three people in ways unimaginable. The first speaker to give a testimony was the young lady. Unbeknownst to me, she had prepared a poem to honor Tina. It didn't take long to realize she was gifted as both a speaker and a creative writer. Her poem pulled at our heartstrings as she read the verses of her rhythmic composition. I don't believe there was a dry eye in the room when she finished. I silently thanked God for using her in such a creative and inspiring manner.

Next up was the lady who worked at the Tyler Cancer Center. She brought with her three pages of notes, although I am sure she could have written much more. She was understandably nervous and not used to speaking in front of large groups. However, I knew God would calm any nervousness she probably felt. Sure enough, once she started talking, the words seemed to flow easily. The following are excerpts from her testimony:

— Four years ago, I met someone who would forever change my life. That person was Tina. I work at the cancer center where she received treatment, and the first day I met her, she was sitting in the waiting room. I noticed she had her Bible with her, and the first words I spoke to her were "I see you brought some good reading material," and she smiled at me and said, "Yes, the best!" From that point on, we loved to talk about our God together.

— Being a Christian for quite a few years now, I thought I had this all figured out. Little did I know what was about to hit me! I go to a small-town Baptist church, and my faith was encased in a box. Anything out of the norm was too much for me to understand or, let's say, believe. Tina always made me see outside of the box! Then finally step out of it!

There are so many stories I could tell you, but the one that grew my faith the most was the one about the gold flakes. Tina came in for her treatment and was sitting in the circle (aka "party circle"). Tina liked to sit there when she was feeling good so she could talk and minister to other patients. Every morning before she would come to the cancer center, she would pray for God to show her who it was she was to minister to that day. God was always faithful to give her someone. The patients looked forward to seeing her. This particular day it was me. She was just glowing that day and could not wait to share with me what God had given her. She opened her hands and said, "Look at the gold." I asked her where this gold was coming from. She said she first noticed the gold flakes on her hands during an intense prayer session at one of her prayer meetings. She indicated that God would give her this blessing sometimes when she would pray. Well, me being a bit like doubting Thomas, I was really searching all over her clothes to see if she had anything with gold sparkle on it. I could not find anything. So I looked at her makeup to see if anything gold and shiny was in her eye shadow. She had not put on her makeup that day. Tina was always in tune with my spirit and was probably seeing me secretly searching for an explanation. In response to my questioning demeanor, she simply took my hands in hers and said, "Let's pray." My heart was racing, and I could certainly feel the Holy Spirit in the room. After an incredibly beautiful prayer, we opened our eyes, and she told me to look at my hands. To my amazement, I had the same gold flakes. The more I rubbed my hands together, the more I got! Wow! At that moment, I forever stepped out of the box I had put my faith in and never looked back in it. Tina showed me that nothing was impossible for God and never should we doubt His glorious gifts! Tina saw God in everything, and because of her never-ending faith, He spoke to her in mighty ways.

— Early this past summer, Tina came to the cancer center once again to start a new treatment. On my usual rounds to the room she received treatment in, she asked me to sit with her and pray about a decision she had to make about her cancer treatment. After the prayer, I had a huge peace come over me, and I told her this. I told her that God only wants what is best for her and not to harm her and give her a great future. Little did I know I was quoting Jeremiah 29:11. She sat straight up in the bed and said, "Oh my gosh! You are quoting Jeremiah 29:11. This is the Scripture God gives me when I need peace about a decision." I was so excited and blessed to be a part of that. For the next three weeks, God gave me Jeremiah 29:11 in many ways, and every time, I would call Tina about how He gave me the Scripture, and we would laugh at God's great sense of humor.

— There is one more story to tell before I close. Just two days after Tina's birthday on August 8, 2008, I was reading my Bible and turned to Romans 12:9–13. It reads as follows: "Love must be sincere. Hate what is evil, cling to what is good. Be devoted to one another in love. Honor one another above yourselves. Never be lacking in zeal, but keep your spiritual fervor, serving the Lord. Be joyful in hope, patient in affliction, and faithful in prayer. Share with the Lord's people who are in need. Practice hospitality." After reading these passages, God's Spirit came over me and asked me who I knew that I could put their name in every sentence. Of course, Tina came to my mind, and I read it again to myself like this: Tina's love is sincere. Tina hates what is evil and clings to what is good. Tina is devoted to one another in brotherly love. Tina honors one another above herself. Tina is never lacking in zeal and keeps her spiritual fervor serving the Lord. Tina is joyful in hope, patient in affliction, and Tina is faithful in prayer. Tina shares with God's people who are in need. Tina practices hospitality. After reading this, I was so excited I had to call her up and share this with her. She was so humble and really was blessed that I could see all of this in her. I was blessed that God showed me how much we should strive to be like the Scripture instructed, and double blessed to meet someone that was.

— In closing, I would like to leave you with these thoughts: (i) Every time you see a rainbow, picture Tina on the other side of it seeing colors brighter than we can ever imagine; (ii) Every time you smell the fragrance of a rose, picture Tina smelling the rose that never dies; and (iii) Every time you see gold, picture Tina walking on the "streets of gold" that never end.

As I pondered the depth of her testimony, I realized her words reflected the spiritual journey of most people. We tend to put our faith in a box and choose not to believe the divine power of God and what He is fully capable of. I firmly believe that God chose those words carefully for her so they would have the greatest impact on those who attended the celebration service. The testimony provided a needed reminder of the things we do that *contain us* and, more importantly, the things we elect not to do that can *sustain us*. It begged the questions I had frequently asked myself in previous years: (1) Do we choose not to believe things we cannot process and understand, or do we examine things through a spiritual lens and rejoice in the signs and wonders that are made known to us? (2) Are we routinely putting into practice the instructions in Romans 12? Praise you, Lord, for these reminders and the use of this servant to deliver the message!

At this point of the service, I didn't think the testimonies could get more powerful. *Wrong!* God was not done yet! The gentleman who followed gave one of the most gut-wrenching testimonies I had ever heard. Although he could have talked for hours, he tried his best to limit his testimony to 30 minutes. I was pleased that he voiced his thoughts and didn't limit God's words that had been given to him. Tina had helped this man and his wife through a difficult time. Their son had disappeared under some unusual circumstances, and they had never been able to determine his whereabouts or even if he was alive. According to this man, Tina had left an incredibly powerful prayer on their answering machine while they were away from their home. The prayer had brought the man and his wife to tears when they listened to it, and he was obviously having difficulty talking about it now. His tears spoke volumes as he summarized the message Tina had left for them. Much of what he said I was completely oblivious to since Tina never solicited any recognition for her actions. She only gave glory to God.

After the man finished speaking, I realized that the service had already been going for more than an hour, and our dear friend and presiding pastor had not even spoken yet. I wondered what he might say that would be a good follow-up to the incredible testimonies we had just heard. The pastor was a true visionary and an insightful speaker. He was always able to explain things in a clear and concise manner. On that day, his words were impactful, as usual. He began his remarks by outlining our calling as followers of Christ. He illustrated how Tina had embraced the tenets of her faith and put them into practice daily. He emphasized that Tina did not hesitate to speak of her love for the Lord and was willing to share the gospel with anyone she met. His message provided an excellent summary of Tina's faith in action and how we are all called to do the same.

After we finished singing "Mighty to Save," the pastor closed the service with his traditional blessing:

> *May the good Lord go*
> before *you to lead you,*
> behind *you to encourage you,*
> beside *you to befriend you,*
> beneath *you to uphold you,*
> above *you to protect you,*
> within *you to inspire you.*

Wow! What a service! I felt energized, and I am sure Tina was looking down at us with a big smile on her face.

As we made our way to the graveside service at the cemetery, I couldn't help but look up at the sky and search for a rainbow.

It was still overcast, and conditions were favorable for light rain. However, there was no evidence of a rainbow anywhere. Perhaps the Lord was waiting for just the right moment at the cemetery to present His panoramic calling card. After the pastor finished his remarks, the trumpeter played a musical salute. The crisp sound of the trumpet through the cemetery provided the perfect musical accompaniment for a colorful, heavenly display. Yes, this must be the moment! Despite the perfect backdrop, however, there was no rainbow.

As we arrived home from the cemetery, I must admit I was slightly downtrodden as I was fully expecting a prolific rainbow to show up on this day. As I pondered this, the phone rang. It was my neighbor. He apologized for not being able to attend the celebration service. However, he said that on his drive home from work, he saw a rainbow in the sky and immediately thought of Tina. I gasped at the news and shouted, “Really?” I then told my neighbor his rainbow sighting made my day. As I hung up the phone, I realized that God had delivered yet another rainbow in honor of Tina. However, in this case, it was meant to be seen by others and not by me. It was a perfect exclamation point on an impactful day!

24

Making an Impact a Year Later

I firmly believe one of our greatest callings in life is to make a positive impact on the world around us. For Christians, that translates to establishing a legacy built on a foundation of faith. Our friends, family, and others in our circle of influence must see us uphold biblical principles and demonstrate brotherly love. Our words and actions should always strive to build one another up, even when our circumstances may suggest otherwise. We may never know what our true impact is on others while we are still on earth. In many cases, the legacy we leave behind will not be known until we have reached our heavenly destination.

The legacy Tina left behind was still felt long after God called her home. The best example of this occurred about a year after her death. The date was Sunday, November 1, 2009. This particular day was a day I could have easily stayed home and crashed. After a late football game on Friday night and an all-day trip to Louisiana on Saturday to watch Grant's high school band participate in a marching competition, I contemplated whether I should drive to Dallas on Sunday and support Andrew in some of his activities (church and hockey). I told Andrew I would try to make it if I was not too tired but would let him know on Sunday morning. I felt pretty good on Sunday when I woke up, so I decided to head west. After texting Andrew that I was headed his way, I journeyed to Dallas to attend the contemporary worship service at St. Luke's Episcopal Church. Andrew was the music leader of the contemporary service and was blessed to have this opportunity while he was still in college. I arrived about 30 minutes before the service started and had a chance to visit with the lead pastor beforehand. I had met the pastor a few times previously and had developed a fondness for him. On that day, he spoke of some of the issues facing his church, and I spoke of similar issues at my church. Even though we were from different church backgrounds, I really enjoyed talking to him and praying with him. After all, we were both part of the body of believers.

After I finished talking to the pastor, I sat down in one of the pews and started reading the worship folder for the service. I noted that this was All Saints' Day. For those of you who are not from a Catholic or highly liturgical church background, All Saints' Day is the day when churches celebrate all the Christian saints, known and unknown. Most churches typically honor their deceased members who have gone home to the Lord during the previous 12 months. As I was scrolling through their list of deceased members, I noticed that Tina's name was included. I thought, *What a nice gesture!* Obviously, Tina and I were not members of this church. No, this was an act of brotherly love for Andrew and his family.

Tina's influence on the service didn't end with a listing in the church bulletin. The pastor spoke on the Beatitudes (Matthew 5) during his sermon and was doing his best to integrate this theme with All Saints' Day. He mentioned that on the way to the church that morning, he thought of all the people he had known who had died the previous year and contemplated who had truly been a "light for Christ" and who had routinely shared the "good news" with others despite their circumstances. Who would be a good modern-day example of someone who hungered and thirsted for righteousness and was pure in heart? He said he thought for a moment, and then his mind focused on the celebration service for Tina he had attended last fall. He then relayed the story told by one of the speakers at Tina's service. It was the story of Tina in the waiting room at the Tyler Cancer Center and her interaction with the lady who worked in the chemo clinic. He relayed how she had approached Tina and made a comment about the book she was holding. Tina immediately held up her Bible and said, "Yes, it's the best book!" The pastor recalled the lady saying that Tina would then use the waiting room time to witness to others. He then remarked, "Here was a person who had gone through numerous chemotherapy programs, radiation treatments, surgeries, and more, and yet took the opportunity to focus on others rather than her own situation. Indeed, here was someone who took up the call for Christ rather than waiting to be called."

Wow! What a testimony a year later! After the service, I relayed some follow-up material to the pastor. I recited part of the "Tina letter" that was read at her parents' 50th wedding anniversary over the previous Labor Day weekend. "Although many will say that I have suffered much in recent years, the truth is I have suffered hardly at all when compared to Christ. It is my faith in God through a personal and loving relationship with

Christ that motivates me each day and carries me forward." After hearing this, the pastor just shook his head, smiled, and said, "Even pastors need encouragement." Yes, there was a reason I was supposed to be at this church on this day. God's Spirit worked in two people's hearts for the benefit of the Kingdom.

Tina's collective impact on the pastor and me didn't stop with All Saints' Day. Another God moment occurred when I again attended a service at St. Luke's on the Sunday when the church was celebrating the pastor's last day there. He was moving on to a church in the San Antonio area. I felt compelled to attend the worship service since I had developed a friendship with him from my frequent visits to the church. He was also the person who hired Andrew to lead the contemporary service in 2008, and I wanted to extend my gratitude for that.

The service marked the first time I had been in the main sanctuary of the church since the contemporary service was always held in the chapel, a separate building. Since this was the pastor's last Sunday, the church held a combined service for contemporary and traditional worshippers. Andrew and his fellow musicians and singers were in the choir loft of the beautiful, rotunda-shaped building with its excellent acoustics. I noticed several times during the service that the pastor looked up toward the balcony when Andrew was playing and singing. A smile was always evident on his face. As the service drew to a close, the pastor positioned himself at the center of the sanctuary and prepared to give the benediction. As he recited the benediction he had prepared, our eyes met briefly while he panned the crowd. At this point, his words became strikingly similar, in fact almost identical to some words Tina had spoken to me just a few days before she went home to the Lord. As he spoke of the need to share the gospel and be a light for Christ, his face became Tina's, and for an instant I thought she was with us in the flesh once again. As he ended the spiritual blessing, I just stood there with tears flowing down my cheeks. Of course, no one else would know the significance of those exact words and the impact they would have on me—*except for God.* As I gathered my belongings and exited the pew I had been sitting in, I realized there was more than one reason I needed to be here today. God used the pastor (again) and the memory of Tina to speak to me about His love for us and our calling to spread the *good news of Jesus Christ*!

As I stood in the receiving line after the service to greet the pastor and extend my best wishes, I pondered what I might say to him. When I finally reached him, I simply told him what had happened during the benediction. The pastor smiled as I started to tear up again and then responded with a story of his own from the previous week's contemporary service, the last such service under his helm. At the end of that service, he reflected on the brief history of the contemporary service and then looked up to the ceiling as he started toward the back of the chapel. When he looked up, he said he saw Tina's face with a big smile on it! The pastor told me he did not tell Andrew about the vision when it occurred. However, he was glad to relay the vision to him today, especially after hearing that I had had a similar vision.

25

The Rainbow Covenant

It would have been easy to assume that the rainbow sightings and other divinely inspired events would subside after Tina's death or, at the very least, my awareness of them would diminish. To the contrary. It seemed my spiritual acuity was sharpened by God from my years of "training" alongside Tina. It seemed not a week went by without seeing a rainbow. I also witnessed many things that were inexplicable and could only have been inspired by God. I am not sure why I had previously been oblivious to so many things in my life. Perhaps God wanted to tune me according to His timetable.

The rainbow sightings continued long after I remarried in 2012 to a wonderful woman, Cindy, who God placed in my life. In fact, the most beautiful and visually compelling rainbow I have ever seen occurred on August 14, 2020. Cindy and I were on day one of a two-day road trip to West Virginia to visit relatives. Our travel itinerary included a stop at the popular Ark Encounter attraction near Williamstown, Kentucky, the following day. As we headed east on Interstate 40 in the early evening, the weather changed from

sunny to partly cloudy with light rain. As we came around a bend in the highway about 30 miles west of Nashville, a jaw-dropping double rainbow popped into our field of vision. The panoramic spectacle was simply breathtaking. Both concentric rainbows were complete, end-to-end images. Its sheer beauty caused me to pull off the interstate onto an exit ramp and take a few pictures with my cell phone. Fortunately, the double rainbow persisted long enough to allow me to take a panoramic picture of it. My heart was pounding as Cindy and I viewed the heavenly painting in the sky.

As I pondered why God chose this place for us to see this amazing double rainbow, I realized that God was blessing our trip through this radiant calling card and at the same time giving us a unique pathway to the Ark Encounter. Indeed, the archway created by the two rainbows seemed to be an entrance gate for a special expedition. Maybe this was God's way of saying, "Follow me, and I will direct your path to the place your heart desires to go." No doubt, I could not wait to see the beautiful re-creation of the famous vessel built by Noah.

When we arrived at the Ark Encounter the next day, I was very excited. We could see the ark from the main parking area about a mile from the attraction. Even at this distance, the size of the structure was impressive. After a short wait, we boarded the shuttle that took us to the main attraction area. Upon exiting the bus and walking a short distance, we were able to get a good side view of the majestic structure. The sheer size of the ark was captivating. The grounds surrounding the ark were neatly landscaped and manicured to provide an even more appealing backdrop for pictures. The ark was simply beautiful.

As we approached the life-size reconstruction of the famous ship, it became apparent that the ark was just as impressive in terms of height and width as it was in length. Clearly, it must have taken Noah a long time to build a structure of that size with the materials and tools he had at his disposal. As we toured the inside of the ark, it was interesting to see the various displays of animals, food, water system management, and exhibits regarding construction details. However, when we got to the top deck of the massive structure, I quickly focused on the Rainbow Covenant exhibit. It marked the covenant God made with Noah as detailed in Genesis 8:20–22. The display contained artwork depicting a rainbow in the background with scenes of Noah and his family, the ark, animals, waves, the sun, a dove with an olive branch, and other images associated with the ark story.

It immediately came to me that this exhibit was why I felt compelled to come to the Ark Encounter in the first place. Not only did the exhibit highlight the covenant God made with Noah, but it also depicted a rainbow that served as a beautiful reminder of that covenant. The rainbow had also served as a symbol of God's covenant with Tina. Just as God promised Noah that He would never again destroy the earth and the life in it, God pledged to Tina that He would never harm her and would instead give her a hope and a future. No wonder Jeremiah 29:11 was given to Tina by the prayer intercessor when she was first diagnosed with cancer. That prayer warrior was simply following God's instructions. The beautiful rainbow that appeared over the cornfield behind her parents' home shortly after was God's confirmation of that covenant.

I had now achieved some sense of closure in this spiritual journey that had spanned more than two decades. Although I may never understand why God does certain things and the manner in which He does them, it is apparent that He has a plan for each of us. In Tina's case, God's plan included a covenant marked by a rainbow.

26

Rainbows to Feathers

Given the significance of rainbows in Tina's life, it made me wonder if God had a special identifier for me. That question was answered shortly after Tina's death. Feathers started showing up every time I thought of Tina or contemplated spiritual matters. At every fork in the road or where I needed to make a decision to determine a path forward, a feather showed up out of nowhere. I frequently saw feathers on the ground, inside our home, at airports, in meetings, and in many other places. The size of the feathers ranged from small to large, depending on the type of bird the feather came from. Many of the feathers were extremely colorful, while others were as white as snow. I surmised that the feathers with vibrant colors were meant to show the beauty of God's Kingdom since they always seemed to show up at times when I felt down or needed a spiritual hug. On the other hand, the white feathers seemed to reflect the purity of Christ, and I usually saw them when I needed to confirm a personal decision. Many feathers were also strategically located as definite route markers highlighting the physical path I should take.

I started collecting the feathers and displayed them in containers on the fireplace mantle. It was not long before the containers were full and I needed a new container. As the years went by, the presence of the feathers continued, and I rejoiced that God was still providing physical evidence that He cared for me!

In 2019, I traveled to Guatemala as part of a mission team from our church. Cindy had gone to the same location in Guatemala the year before as part of a medical mission team. As our group traveled to a mountainous area of the country about 30 minutes from Antigua, I began to wonder if I was really doing what God wanted me to do at this stage of my life. The next day as I sat outdoors in a chair listening to a Hispanic man give his testimony and an incredible story of survival and why he felt called to help lead this particular ministry, I kept wondering, *God, am I really in the right place?* For some reason, I didn't have peace about the decision to be there. No sooner had I wrestled with myself regarding this thought that I looked down and saw a large feather. My mouth dropped open as I examined the visual confirmation from God. *Okay, Lord. Message received! It seems you provide spiritual markers for me at international locations, too!* From that point on, I was richly blessed by this unique ministry opportunity. I will forever cherish the time I spent with the people from the local community. I don't know if I made an impact on them, but they were a definite blessing to me. The special *pluma* made the trip home to Texas, and I added it to the collection. Not only did it serve as a physical reminder of the time spent in Guatemala, but its presence alongside the other feathers symbolized the fact that as Christians, we are part of a larger group that shares a common bond.

As I reflected on all the experiences depicted by the feathers in the various containers, I was reminded that it was not that long ago that I was blind to all of this. Thankfully, God was quite direct with Tina and me about His presence. The rainbows, feathers, and other divinely inspired signs strengthened our faith, sharpened our spiritual vision, and cemented our passion to share the gospel.

Time to tell others . . .

Which Path, Lord?

Which path, Lord
Is right for me?
I have been in prayer
And down on my knees.

A sign from above
Is what I seek,
A vision or word
To touch my cheek.

Behold, you have spoken
Now I clearly see,
A heavenly rainbow
Meant just for me.

I will go forth now
And proclaim your glory,
Use me, Lord,
To tell your story.

—William A. Heimbaugh

Tina Teter Heimbaugh
1961-2008

Wife, Mother, Daughter, Sister, Friend, Lover,
Spiritual Partner, Evangelist, Disciple of Christ

About the Author

William ("Bill") Heimbaugh is a husband, father, papa, mentor, and devoted follower of Jesus Christ. He is an ordained deacon in a Baptist church and a trained Stephen Minister. He lives in the Waco, Texas, area and enjoys outdoor activities, traveling, and watching hockey. Bill is semiretired but still supports an engineering company he helped start in 2004. His career in the energy industry includes leadership positions in engineering, business development, and management. He has written three technical papers during his professional career, as well as numerous newsletter blogs, press releases, website material, and training manuals. On a personal level, Bill has written several poems for commemorative family events.

www.ingramcontent.com/pod-product-compliance
Lightning Source LLC
LaVergne TN
LVHW010100110826
845155LV00028B/425

* 9 7 8 1 9 5 3 3 0 0 7 7 5 *